MW01289421

INFERTILITY SUCKS, YOU DON'T!

~

SHANNON WOOTEN

Certain names and identifying characters have been changed, whether or not so noted in the text, and certain characters and events have been compressed and reordered.

www.LifewithShannon.com

Designed by Shawna Poliziani.

For Scott, thank you for reminding me whom I was when I had forgotten.
For Ella, you are never alone as long as you love yourself.

All battles are first won or lost in the mind.
-JOAN OF ARC

INFERTILITY SUCKS, YOU DON'T!

PRELUDE

~

I've always known Shannon would write a book. I didn't know what the content of the book would be, but she's always been an incredible writer. She's always had a way with words and I've watched her spend more than 2 and a half years perfecting the words in this book. I'm not surprised that she wrote an entire book, but perhaps the content is. Perhaps that's because the whole situation is a surprise all together.

I want to warn you that what you're about to read is a real, raw, and honest document of our experience with infertility. I also want to tell you that at times it felt like I was watching this unfold as if it wasn't happening to me too; it felt like a movie or a story instead of real life.

It was a Tuesday when I came home from work and Shannon told me she was going to have surgery … on Friday. I'm not even sure if I knew she was going to see a doctor beforehand, it sounds bad but I honestly can't remember. What I do remember is that she had been telling me that she just felt like something wasn't right and it's why we weren't getting pregnant despite trying for a year. The surgery felt fast - I hadn't even met this doctor in person yet but I agreed because Shannon was so adamant that she HAD to do this. And then it began.

For the next several years we were in a fight we didn't sign up for. At first I thought we signed up for a tag team match, but as the fight went on I realized Shannon was in a Royal Rumble by herself. I should have been better so many times. There are multiple times I wasn't there when I could and should have been but simply didn't know how hard she was fighting. I knew everyone around us couldn't understand what we were going through, but it was a major wake up call when I realized that not even I understood what she was going through. I wish I could take every one of those instances back. I'll never feel like those times weren't my biggest failures in life so far.

I watched her give herself so many shots for so many months. I hated it even more when there were shots I had to give her because she couldn't do them herself. She never complained though, not once. She was determined that this was going to work and every time we didn't get pregnant, she was convinced the next one would. Hell, I felt that way too. I'm almost always an optimist, I can't help it. The glass is always half full - there's no other way for me to see it.

The more times the pregnancy test came back negative, the more frustrated Shannon became and I watched her slip into a version of herself I'd never met before. And my optimism wasn't helping, if anything, it was making it worse.

I stopped saying things I would have normally said. I would do anything to avoid a fight, but everything I said would seemingly start some sort of fight. We were in a perpetual fight over everything, and none of the things we were arguing about mattered at all. After another trivial fight for the 100th time, I finally broke.

I remember absolutely knowing without a doubt that the next sentence I was about to say was going to make it worse but I didn't really feel like I had a choice anymore. I said. "Shannon, you're depressed." I was right, but it was worse than I thought it would be. It would be a few days before we were communicating normally again and I probably picked the wrong time to say those three words to her. I'm also not sure there was ever going to be a right time to say them. Ultimately, I can look back to that conversation as a turning point for us.

It was probably a few months later that Shannon sat me down and said "I release you." Release me from what? I wasn't asking to be released from anything. I didn't want to be released. But for whatever reason, Shannon felt like she needed to tell me I could leave. I could go find someone else to try and have kids with as if I wanted to have kids with anyone other than her in the first place.

Technically, it was my fault. I've never been a great communicator so I probably wasn't clear when we were dating and I said that if she didn't want to have kids it would be a deal breaker for me. We actually broke up over it, but I think it was only for a couple of hours. I knew I wanted to have kids and whomever I married would need to want to have kids with me. Again, no one prepares you that you might not be *able* to have kids.

I get what was she was saying and I understand why she felt the need to tell me that. The truth is that I was ready to stop the fight long before Shannon was. Not because I don't want kids, but because I'm not willing to lose my wife in the process of having kids.

Shannon is my rock. Everything I've achieved is mostly because of her. She's my muse, my everything. Turns out I was wrong, I don't need kids. I don't even want them if the expense of getting them is watching Shannon put herself through more needles, more doctors just going through the motions treating us both like a number instead of a human, and more heartache over something that's completely out of our control.

Some people will say we are giving up - and I'm cool with that. Shannon is too. This book isn't going to give you some secret about how to get pregnant. It also doesn't have a fairy tale ending where we get pregnant and have multiple kids. Not everyone gets that ending, but this book is for everyone that can relate to going through the struggle. It's everything we wished we had known before. It's everything we wanted someone to tell us.

These few paragraphs are just a glimpse of our struggle from my perspective. Shannon is the writer and can do a much better job of finding the right words. Like I said, I'm not the greatest communicator.

I'm so proud of this book. I'm so proud of her hard work. I'm so proud she's my wife. She's incredible. After you read this book, I think you'll agree.

~

What started as an attempt at journaling turned into a heart wrenching account of what would become one of my most life changing experiences to date. I started writing to help clear the burdensome energy that existed in my mind and plagued my heart, but as I continued to write, what began as a cathartic experience for me, evolved into my love letter to you.

PROLOGUE
JULY 8, 2018

~

As the doctors prepped me for laparoscopic surgery and wheeled me out of the pre-operating room, I watched the faces of my family fade off into the distance. I had them in the pre-op room with me as I awaited my first serious surgical procedure, because that is what they and I do. I could tell they were hopeful, and yet concerned. I could tell, because while their words were filled with certainty and inspiration, their eyes said they were fearful and confused.

I heard their words of support and I felt their love, but no one could deny the confusion in their eyes. I understood confusion surrounding this whole situation and their questions about infertility, why this step was necessary and how does laparoscopic surgery go, what does it take to heal and when would I get what I want from this; when would I get my baby? I understood all their questions because I shared them.

I remember the only person in the room that day who seemed unbothered and not at all worried was Mom. She has that brave, protective, and certain way about her when it comes to her kids, like the Momma Bear from Disney's Brave. If you have never seen it, you should. Since she is the Momma Bear, I'm sure you have discerned that makes me the daughter, Merida. I don't deny what a real jerk-off Merida can be at times and I don't deny how that parallels to me, but just like the mom in the movie, my Momma Bear loves me anyway.

My mom, like the Momma Bear, acts like only moms can. She has the ability to express herself in this superhuman way that makes you believe everything will be fine. It's like she reaches into your soul with her eyes, grasps your worries with words, and instantly, penetrates your fear. She has that Mom-like ability to make you know that you are so loved, so the only possible outcome is for everything to be all right.

Mom was the last person to say anything to me that day. As everyone else left the room, she walked alongside the bed as the doctors wheeled me out and into a future that would forever change me, my life, who I was, how I live, and what I show-up as in it.

I remember her saying, "You got this." Which was immediately followed by a pause that could not have been longer than 2.5 seconds, but felt like 10 minutes, as she stared lovingly into my eyes.

Then, she said, "You can do this!" Which was followed by another pause that had to have been brief, but felt like an eternity, as she stared harder and knowingly, into my soul.

And, as I began to tear up, my voice shook as I said, "Yeah." Which truthfully, I didn't believe or know, but I think I said it for her and for Scott, who was standing behind her crying.

As the bed turned a corner, and the space between us grew, she intentionally stepped in front of Scott, so I could no longer see him. Not to block him out or to create a distance between him and me, but so I could only see her, confidently, determinately, and forcefully, nodding her head as she said, "I love you", and then, in all her mom glory, raised her arms into the air like she had just won a marathon. It made me laugh of course, but it also made me cry, because I was afraid and they all knew it.

As I saw her fade off into the distance, I remember thinking I am scared, but I believe her, because she is my mom. She is my insides. Hell, I'm physically *her* insides. I believe her because I don't believe there is anyone in the world who knows a child quite like his or her mother does. No offense, Dads, you're fucking fantastic, too. But, my mom is the definition of modest bravery. She is strong, intentional, loving, sensitive, and well, she's my mom.

What I didn't know is that when she said, with love, "You got this" that she meant whatever happened, good or bad, I would be able to come out on the other side of everything that is infertility. She would be right.

I didn't know that when she said "You can do this" with an intense knowing, that she meant no matter how long it takes or what obstacles the next phase of the journey entailed, that I would be able to withstand it's intensity and preserve. She was also right.

I didn't know that when she raised her arms into the air like she had just won an Olympic Gold Medal, that she was actually already cheering for who I was on the other side of this. It would be her cheering for the win I would receive in realizing who I needed to be to survive infertility and who the future Shannon would become. Mom, I'm sure you've waited forever to hear this, but for all of it, you were right.

Knowing that you got this, you can do this, and that the person you want to be on the other side of infertility is possible, is exactly what I will teach you to notice in this book. You will find harsh truths, awareness that you may not like, and even a realization that you are perpetuating your pain, but at the end of it, you will decide if you can find acceptance or not. You will decide if you are this disease or you are someone who is allowing themselves to be devalued by it.

On July 8, 2013, I received laparoscopic surgery to discover stage IV endometriosis, polycystic ovaries, and a benign tumor inside my uterus that would require a D & C procedure, adhesion extraction, and leave me with 4 surgical scars. For those who don't know, a D & C , is a procedure in which the cervix is dilated so that the uterine lining can be scraped with a spoon shaped instrument to remove abnormal tissues. That day changed my life, who I was, my future, everything about me that I had ever thought or believed to be true, and it was hard, lonely, and totally confusing. That paragraph, while short, does not describe the sequence of events that would follow. This book however, will.

What happened over the years that followed would shock the living hell out of me and while I can't speak for my husband, I will go out on a limb and say that it was probably shocking for him too. What would happen is that while in the process of trying to create life, I would engage in a battle for my own. I would become suicidal, scared, enraged, fearful, pissed off, depressed, and hate no one more than myself, but I would not only survive, I would thrive.

I survived but I wouldn't say that it was a walk in the park.

I wish I could tell you that I was brave throughout our struggle with infertility, but I wasn't. There were moments of desperation in which I wanted it to end. All of it. Life, living, trying to endure an existence that felt wrong, hard, painful, flooded with blame, shame, guilt, and fear. I wanted to die and I hated myself for thinking so, but also because I couldn't seem to make myself stop thinking it.

Infertility was destroying me. The struggle of trying to get pregnant was destroying me. My mind and the blame I felt was destroying me. I had let all of it take over everything I was and I was tired of it.

Prior to infertility, I wasn't afraid. I didn't feel broken. I wasn't confused about who I was. I knew who the fuck I was! It wasn't someone who lets anyone or anything make choices for her, and this *thing* wasn't going to be in charge of me anymore. It wasn't going to put this "Baby, in a corner". I wanted to come out of hiding. I knew I wouldn't be the same, but that didn't scare me. In fact, it made me confident that if I could come back from this, then I would only be stronger. It was time to bring Shannon back to life.

I was done feeling sorry for myself. I was done lashing out at people, crying in restrooms, or hating on other women's pregnant bellies and babies. They're babies for Christ's sake! I was Shannon Fucking Wooten! I love Tinkerbell, laughing, sex, romantic comedies, dancing, singing, people, and believing that I can do any motherfucking thing. I am brave, because that is who I was raised to be, and that is who I was going to need to be to love me back to life. That is who I was going to need to be to find out who I am after infertility, because I can't go back now.

I can't change the past, but I can work on who I am in the present, because I know who I want to be in the future. I know who I will have to be in order to bring me back to life. I will need to stop acting like this is something I've done to myself, and love on me like I would a best friend. I will have to get comfortable with the uncomfortable and I will have to understand that in life there is a lot we will have no control over and find peace with not knowing.

I don't know if I'll ever have a baby. I don't know if I'll find answers to infertility. I don't know who I will be on the other side of this, but all I need to know is that I am committed to being there. I know that I am not going anywhere. I know that while this disease fucking sucks, on July 8th, I went into surgery to fight this thing because I am brave, I am love, and I don't suck, infertility does.

CHAPTER 1: LIFE ISN'T A FAIRYTALE.

~

For most of my professional life I have been a Project Manager. I got paid to keep things organized, create a sense of urgency, and manage open lines of communication. I am the person who takes control and leaves no room for ambiguity. I like structure; deadlines, rules and clarity, and I have heard a time or two that I do not excel "living in the gray". I don't exactly know what that means and after 30+ years on this planet I still don't. It's not something you can define by looking it up in the dictionary, either. Trust me. I've looked. My literal self finds the comparison incorrect because my favorite colors are black, white, and you guessed it – gray, but people have their opinions. Hell, this whole book is full of mine.

In addition to being "gray", I've also been told that my confidence and ability to set an expectation is an asset. I communicate clearly and sometimes so clear it is to a profanity filled and sarcastic fault. I've heard that my "do it yourself" Type-A personality, is consistent, inspiring, and motivating. Others have said that my directness comes across as dominating or arrogant, and it leaves them feeling dejected or overlooked. All things considered, I see me as being myself. My intention is hardly ever to be dismissive, so while I don't know that I disagree with people's assessments one-way or the other, like I said, everyone has their opinions.

If you're asking me, I've always felt an addictive energy when comes to conquering a problem, situation, or task. I see the issue, ingest it as manageable, and become laser focused on executing until it is resolved, settled, or done. I have never taken a personality test or researched the differences between personality types, up until about 2.5 seconds ago, but I have always been told mine is Type-A.

According to Wikipedia, a type-A personality is a temperament characterized by excessive ambition, aggression, competitiveness, drive, impatience, need for control, someone who is focused on quantity over quality, and has an unrealistic sense of urgency. I can get down with that. I can, because I relate to it, or at least I did. Does that mean you have to? No. Do what you like, but for the sake of *this book* we're moving forward with the above, because Wikipedia and I say so.

I can admit that a Type-A personality sounds like me or at least I can say who I was prior to infertility. Looking back, I was all, if not most, of what Wikipedia describes; ambitious, competitive, impatient, controlling, laser focused on having everything "done yesterday", and sometimes known as "a dog with a bone". While I've never been 100% certain if the dog and bone comparison is any better than not being able to exist in the "gray", I accept it, as long as I am a gorgeous German Shepherd.

In my professional life, I see a clear connection to a Type-A personality. I can admit that I am familiar with having a one-track mind. I am focused on the timetable that I want, and having all pieces play-out in the way that I want it. Managing time, people and expectations is something I am very accustomed to. I'm aware that saying so makes me sound like a self-righteous brat, and I might agree if I had said I believe its cool to be a dick about it, but I didn't. Don't be a dick.

What I'm saying is, once I'm committed to something, I tend to be concerned only with it, and once I align myself to a thought, feeling, or action, that commitment stays until whatever is in play is achieved, implemented, or done. I like done. Done is good.

In my personal life, I am a true Gemini. Not only because my birthday is in June, but because some might say I have multiple personality disorder, to which I would gladly accept as a compliment. Thank you!

Sprinkled into my personal life are bits and pieces of a control freak persona. I manage the bills, clean every nook and cranny of the house on my hands and knees, create grocery lists by recipe, color coordinate my closet, get my roots touched up every 4-weeks to the day, and remind Scott, aka my husband, when he needs to handle the kitty litter and laundry, and maybe, also when he forgets.

On the other side of that insanity, which I say lovingly because it drives me insane to be that tightly wound, I love leisure, spontaneity, freedom, change, swear words, rock n' roll, poetry, horror movies and Tinkerbell. Some days I love keeping it all together and others I choose not to put on underwear because... well, freedom! I'm equal parts "Mommy Dearest" and a free spirited rebel tied up in a little black box with some poetry, spikes, leather, butterflies, lace, music and a neon pink bow. I'm not the "what you see is what you get" kind of gal. I'm more the "who is showing-up today" woman.

Maybe my hyper focused self beckons the uncontrolled foul-mouth Queen for some levity, relaxation, and a bit of party. I don't know? Quite frankly, there are too many other things I'd rather do than figure it out. Call it ignorance. Call it liberation. Your guess is as good as mine.

What I know is, what shows-up is always different depending on the day or circumstance. Ultimately, I like that unpredictability, and for the most part, I like me. I can unequivocally attribute my self-esteem to my father, who always taught me that respecting yourself is just about the best thing you can do for you and everyone around you, next to respecting others. Thanks, Dad!

I don't like to take life too seriously. Something I can also blame on my parents, who taught me at a young age that Walt Disney and Mickey Mouse are two of the coolest things on the planet. They taught me to believe that there is some magic to every moment and that I can create whatever life I want. I'd like to say all the things they taught me seeped into my brain and stuck like glue, but let's be real. How much of what we learn do we follow to a T? Also, in my opinion, every good kid has a part of them that goes rogue.

I can admit that the rebel in me likes to sway from the straight and narrow, and for that, this is the first of many times I will apologize to my parents. Sorry, Mom and Dad; you did a fantastic job creating a human that is not a murderer, gives to those in need, and is considerate of old people. They also encouraged me to say "Excuse Me", stand-up for myself, stand-up for others, lead with love, use my brain before my beauty, and if I don't have anything nice to say then I shouldn't say it at all. That last part might've gotten a little lost in translation. Perhaps, that's why I find it acceptable to respond to something I don't like with "suck all the dicks" versus "well, that was unpleasant". Not because I can't think of anything "intelligent" to say, which the assertion by the way irks me, but because sometimes that is what my brain says and sometimes I just want to say what I think.

The rebel in me finds consistent proper behavior to be... well, boring! I also find people who diminish the intelligence of others based on their use of swear words to be boring! I have a Master's Degree in Communications and if I choose to use the word fuck over darn, then that is my prerogative. It is also yours to put me in a box and define me as crass or simpleminded for doing so, but I don't have to be in that box with you.

That said, I think life should be fun, because my Mommy and Daddy said so! Gosh, that felt good. Not really, okay, kind of. Regardless of my parental justification, I say this because I think we as people feel an allegiance to follow the rules. Believe me. The irony of typing this to you is a lot even for my controlling, ass, but I believe it's true.

Most of us are so worried about saying or doing the wrong thing that we walk around with a perpetual stick up our butt, and all it gives us in return is anxiety, an inferiority complex, and a constant obsession to compare or measure ourselves by the standards of others, and possibly, a wedgie. I know, because I've done this. Trying to manage everything, predict the future, or plan for the unplanned is exhausting and by the way, not fun! Even if you say it is, I'm going to tell you that you're a liar. It's not fun!

I want to be clear that when I say I don't take life too seriously, it doesn't mean that is why I use swear words. No. That's just a little tangent I went on to prepare you for the amount of profanity that will be used in this book. I say it because with or without the use of expletives life is already serious. We're born. We get a finite amount of time to live and then we die. Hello – let's have some fun! Let the lid off a little and stop flinching when someone uses four-letter words from the dictionary.

What's more serious? Being born with a ticking time clock called aging, that reminds you the older you get you're actually expiring. Not *maybe* you will expire. No. It is a definite. You *will* expire.

Death is a serious fact, but I think it is something we can only value by looking at it as an opportunity to see all that is possible. I'm not telling you to live in fear of dying or to pretend everything is sunshine, whiskey and chocolate; "...these are a few of my favorite things", but that there is a necessity to create your own rules, be reckless sometimes, search for the good in everything, and celebrate whenever possible.

Like I said, I think rebellion lives alongside the fact that someday we are going to die. There is so much that can go wrong or unexpectedly occur that it is imperative we remind ourselves to chill out and embrace the magic. Loosen that bun, Barb! Unbutton that top button, Tony! Say a curse word, indulge in an extra brownie, or do something every once in a while just because it feels good, and not because you know it is the safe, predictable, thing you always do. No. Do something that really throws you off, knocks the wind out of you, and asks, "What the fuck was that, Sally?!" Do it because it is available to you and as real as the fact that you will cease to exist one day. Do it because living means believing in the possible.

We live in a world where anything is possible and I believe that's what living is all about; believing our own hype, the possibility we have to create a future we love, and having fun. Do I think amazing things happen every day? Yes. Do I think that life will always be fun? No. Life is full of possibility, but it isn't a fairytale. There is no such thing as control, shit goes wrong and there is disappointment. I know this. I've experienced it.

I have a deafening awareness around disappointment. I'd like to believe we all do from a very early age. Otherwise, the first word from the mouth of every toddler I've ever met wouldn't be, "No!" I think we say no because we don't want to be controlled, and we don't want to be controlled, because we don't want to be disappointed, and we don't want to be disappointment, because ultimately, we believe there is a possibility that we can get what we want, and the possibility to get what we want allows us to believe we can avoid or resolve disappointment if we work hard enough.

~

Contrary to those who like to live in the land of the "sure thing", possibility exists. It is what allows us to get out of bed in the morning and believe that it is going to be a great day. It is what allows us to be equal parts reserved and the life of the party. It is what makes us believe that if we work hard enough, there will be an equal or greater payoff. It is what makes people quit their jobs to start their own business. It gives us hope. It gives us determination. It gives us freedom of spirit. It's magic and it gives us the balls to do the hard shit while believing it will turnout okay. However, it is also a curse because we have that awareness. We know that every day has the potential to be great, but when it doesn't, and quite often it does not, we are disappointed.

What gave me hope and disappointment around possibility? Motherhood.

I'm not the kind of gal who imagined herself with a family. It was not something I wanted since birth, or even in my early twenties. In fact, I didn't have any real commitment to commitment. I was happy with Shannon just as she was. In fact, I was indifferent about marriage for a long time too. No. I don't have Mommy and Daddy issues... at least, I don't think I do. I'm not the product of divorce. I believe I am capable of love. There's no secret reason other than it was unimportant to me and it didn't matter. I was more concerned with having someone who I loved, love me back. The paperwork was irrelevant.

I remember the first time my husband told me he wanted to marry me.

He said something like, "I want to get married. I could be married to you."
I said, "No."

It was several years of having this same conversation, and me uttering something like "I'll let you know" before my husband got fed-up and decided that marriage was important to him. The commitment was important to him. The bond of marriage meant something to him and he wanted all of that with me.

Regardless of what he said or didn't, I wasn't sure if I wanted to be married, but I was sure that he was my person. He was and is my very best friend and soul mate. I didn't and don't want anyone else. I decided that him telling me what he needed, which was to have his choice reflected on paper, wasn't much different than me choosing him and seeing that love as the special once in a lifetime kind. I didn't need the paper, but I wanted him. Needless to say, we got hitched. Now my last name is a hyphenate, 13 letters long, and signing a check is a bitch!

Similar to being married, having children was not something I thought about because I didn't want it. I was perfectly happy in my self-absorbed, independent, carefree, married life, with our fur babies. I didn't need anything else. Yet, the older I got the more I started to consider having a child with my husband. The more I thought about it, the more I likened to it, and the more I likened to it, the idea both terrified and enlightened me.

Motherhood took quite a bit of time, growth and consideration to see as a viable option for me. My husband seemed open to it almost immediately, but for me it was a challenge. There was so much unknown around it. A lot of planning needed to occur and given my personality, that meant I needed to have everything "just right". It was an unpredictable, big, commitment, and one that I didn't know how to fully prepare for.

Decision making for me is pretty standard. Either I want to do something and I'm all in, or I don't and I'm all out. That's not to be confused with not wanting something and then changing your mind. I view those as two very different things, because I believe in timing. If I decide something is "off the table" then it is off forever, or until further notice. Motherhood was that sort of thing for me. For the better part of 30 years it was not an option, then one day I had decided it was something I could be into and from that moment forward I was committed.

Motherhood was something that allowed me to see change was possible. Like I said before, I always believed in it. I just never had the opportunity to see it as it was happening. The thought of becoming a Mother transformed me from independent and carefree, Shannon, to a version of myself that immediately considered how I was taking care of my body and my personal well-being each day for something other than me.

My reaction to having a child was instantaneous from the moment I decided and from that moment, it wasn't an "if" scenario, it was a reality. It wasn't a "when" I become a Mom mentality; it was I am already a Mom, so when I say real, I mean that in my mind me having a child was absolute.

Motherhood is something that I decided with my husband, whom I'll share how amazing, handsome, and delicious a human he is later. For now, I want you to know that he is the only reason I want to bring a child into this world. He is the only person I will ever want to do it with and it is because he is such an exceptional man that I can't think of anyone cooler, smarter, or downright sexy to procreate with.

Having a baby became a dream that we created together. It came to be because I love him and who I am with him so much, that growing the love we have into a whole human only seemed right. While it scared me, it changed me, and the decision we made together took on a whole new meaning for me. A meaning that was intense, loving, and exhilarating, and because of that it held a lot of weight.

Having a baby held so much weight, because it was not just my dream. It was our dream. There is no one I'd rather give this gift to. There is no one I'd rather give this gift to me. I hate to admit that there was an immediate pressure to conceive, but it is true. There was. We had decided something; so naturally, I was ready for it to happen yesterday. We were in it, focused, ready to create and make it happen. It was something that we were doing together, but I had to carry and deliver it into life for us. My body would change, my habits would change, my health and well-being would support two, and while I was up for the challenge, the awareness around that responsibility was substantial.

Sure. I worried about what kind of pregnant woman I would be, but not more than I celebrated in the excitement of it. However, the excitement was short-lived. Almost as immediately as we had agreed to have a child, we discovered why it could be difficult. Call it intuition. Call it fear. Call it whatever you want, but after a short period of trying to conceive, the whole reason we found out about infertility is because I had a "feeling" something was wrong. Later we will dive further into what lead me to see an infertility specialist for the first time, but when I discovered that I was the reason conceiving would be difficult, it felt like I not only let my husband down, but I had failed myself and removed the hope of possibility.

Despite my heart saying Yes to Motherhood, because my body was saying No, I had killed our dream. I was saying No to my husband, to me, and to our future family. I created the disappointment and it changed my personality. It changed me.

The magical, have fun, live life, and believe in possibility side of me went quiet. At the time, it felt like she had died or went into a perpetual "time-out". I was numb and unavailable for anything other than infertility damage control. Everything became about trying to fix, manage, or lead this situation. There was no more time for carelessness, free spirited freedom, or chilling-out. All those things went to the back burner and I went on autopilot with one focus, Motherhood.

~

Being accustomed to getting what I want and in the way that I wanted created a certain level of expectation that wasn't based on what's possible. It was based on believing that with enough effort, management, and being persistent until things went my way. It allowed me to keep going and believe that having a child would happen for us. However, it also created a sense of responsibility that made me feel like I had to keep going until I got what I wanted. I was my own worst enemy.

Yes. Getting pregnant was the goal, but month after month of failed pregnancy, having a baby soon became a job and with that it became an obsessive burden. I couldn't stop the cycle of trying, because I was the problem. I had to fix it! No matter the amount of decline I began to see in my well-being, which we will explore more later, I had to keep going.

In my mind, hard work equaled pay-off, and if I didn't continue to work hard at this, then the failure, disappointment, and the death of our dream, was my fault. Month after month, visit after doctors visit, time spent watching my ovaries produce egg cell growth with what could potentially be our child, allowed hope and possibility to exist. What followed when my body rejected the process by passing clots the size of silver dollars, and feeling the pain that accompanied discharging a thick, black, endometrium, alienated me from my femininity and from my spirit. I know that I wasn't dying and that I didn't, but each period felt like a part of me had died and my strength, my soul and my identity went with it.

As this month-to-month cycle repeated, fault, blame and guilt became my primary emotions. I saw myself as defective and infertility as a punishment for getting this "womanhood thing" wrong. I had started to equate womanhood with motherhood and began to feel like my insides were jumbled-up, because I wasn't the "right kind" of woman. To me being a woman had become connected to having a baby. They became interchangeable and if I couldn't have a baby, then I didn't see myself as a female. I didn't know what I was anymore. I just felt responsible.

I didn't attribute feeling responsible for our struggle to feeling remorseful for it. I took it on as my problem, my issue to resolve, or circumstance to manage. I wasn't looking for sympathy because I didn't know what it would be for? For my broken insides or my broken heart? I didn't want people to feel sorry for me. I saw my responsibility to infertility as a scarlet letter, as a burden I needed to bear, and as a penitence to serve because my body was defective and I couldn't figure it out.

Don't misunderstand me, I was sorry. I was so painfully sorry for my husband that crying multiple times per day in isolation became the norm. Truthfully, I didn't know what I was sorry for? I didn't ask for this. All I wanted was to succeed at doing what seemingly all women should be able to do. So, when we learned I had a disease that would make this "womanhood thing" hard or even impossible, I was confused. No one had talked to me about infertility before. No doctor in the history of having Gynecologists peek into and poke around in my vagina had ever mentioned it. I didn't understand why after 30 years of living, infertility was suddenly happening to us. Despite all the confusion, I knew my body wasn't doing what we needed it to do and I felt lost, alone, and ashamed.

I viewed my symptoms relating to infertility as a right of passage to hate myself and for others to hate me too. My mind was not willing to accept that something was happening to me, and it was not an at fault scenario. I saw myself as the reason we couldn't conceive and because of that I took ownership. I accepted guilt, because I felt accountability needed to be placed somewhere. The more I settled into these emotions, the less room there was for forgiveness, adjustment, or compassion.

When having a baby started to seem more like a long shot, and less like a possibility, I started to lose myself. Everything Shannon had been up to that point was being challenged. All the beliefs I had about possibility started to feel like a blessing that I was unworthy to receive. Everything I thought was true about my ability to create a life that I could love started to dwindle. The world I had believed in changed.

I went from believing "the world is your oyster", and "life is what you make of it", to life is a prison and my body is the enemy. I was lost. The less I saw myself as someone diagnosed with a disease, the less I saw Shannon as a woman, and the more I became nothing more than a useless shell mangled by infertility.

An indistinct line had developed between it and me. I had evolved from someone who believed that life has limitless possibility, that I was responsible for my fate, that I could manage, create, or take-on whatever lied before me, to believing I was broken and living in punishment.

Infertility became who I was. It is how I identified to myself.
"Hi! I'm Shannon. I have infertility."
I don't' say that in gest. I say that in sincerity. My identity was infertility and there was nothing else to me. It was me, and I was it, and that is just the beginning.

~

This book is a love letter to anyone struggling with infertility. It is not a solution, but a real, raw, and painful account of what it's like to survive this disease through the eyes, ears, and soul of someone who lives with it. There is happiness beyond this. You can create it. This is not the end.

This is a love letter to myself. To the girl who I was before all this fucked-up shit went down. It is an ode to the person she was and what she had to grow through in order to survive. I love you. I thank you. Forgive yourself. You are a badass.

This is a love letter to myself. To the woman, wife, lover, nurturer, sister, daughter, and human I am now. You did what you never thought possible. I love you. You amaze me. You are whole, complete, and a fucking rockstar!

This is my love letter to you. To those struggling to find who you are now and freedom from the barriers that keep the pain in. This is a note that you do not have to do this on your own. You are not alone. You can get through this. Forgive yourself. You are a badass.

This is my love letter to you. To those struggling alongside someone who has been diagnosed with symptoms related to infertility and feels pushed out. This is a note that there is no right or wrong way to navigate this with them. You are entitled to have feelings about this too. You are not alone. Forgive yourself. You are lovable.

This book is not a fairytale. It is not a story where I tell you everything worked out in the end for me, because it didn't. I didn't get my happy ending, at least not the one that I almost killed myself for, but I survived and I couldn't love myself more for it.

This is a book about choice. It is about what happens when you stop seeing yourself as whom you *should be* and start seeing yourself as whom you are *willing* to become.

This is a book about possibility and what that looks like from both sides of the coin. It considers hope for the good, but also gives grace to things, behaviors, or actions that might turnout not so good. It is about creating a positive outcome when things go wrong and seeing the love within you to forgive and take accountability to move forward.

You may not get what you want out of this book. Hell, you may not get what you want out of life. What I got was unplanned. What I got was something that I never imagined. What I got was a version of myself that no longer sees me as being two separate people. What I got was a transformation of self, life, love, discovery, anger, resentment, fear, courage, failure, pain, isolation, greed, envy, rage, connection, sorrow, grief, healing and pain.

What I got was release from infertility, and if nothing else, I hope you can too.

CHAPTER 2:
WHAT IS "HAPPILY EVER AFTER"?

O nce upon a time, in a life similar to yours, a fairytale was told. In this story, someone who strangely resembles you accepted the idea of living "happily ever after." You know the one? Boy meets girl. Girl eludes boy. Boy gets girl after some daredevil act of triviality wins over girl, boy and girl get married, have two beautiful kids and buy a house in the suburbs with a nice white picket fence. If your fairytale includes more boy gets boy, or girl gets girl, then move forward with that.

What we're analyzing here is less about the specifics of your sexual attraction. Do you. This is about your expectation for the way life should have unfolded and your feelings of disappointment because it hasn't. This is about the story you have latched onto with a Kung Fu like grip and have refused to let go. This is about you having invested in the possibility of living a storybook life and, now that it feels like you're not, you are using what seems like an unhappy ending to keep you stuck and prevent you from overcoming feelings of rejection.

Not sure if this sounds like you? Let me say this as plainly as possible. If living "happily ever after" has driven most of your reality, then you bought into a fairytale and believed that your story would happen exactly as you imagined. There is no shame in admitting this. Hell, I'm pretty sure 95% of the world does this, so relax. The only issue with any of it comes when life has other plans and you refuse to adapt.

No worries! This is all manageable. I don't need to be sitting right next to you to hear the thoughts of doubt currently swirling through your head. "That's easy for her to say!" "She doesn't understand what I've gone through."

One of my favorite anonymous quotes is, "You want to make life laugh, tell it your plans." It's so true. Nothing in life can be arranged to a T, and yet, we continue to try and if it falls apart we can become paralyzed by thoughts of, "How did this happen" or "What did I do wrong?" When the path to "happily ever after" takes a detour and requires you to re-write your story, who is in shock? You are! Why are you disappointed? Fairytales are both things you tell yourself and things you're willing to believe.

All fairytales have adversity but generally everything works out in the end. In life, this isn't always true. There isn't always a happy ending and true pain can come from that truth. Ultimately, outside the confines of your favorite story and inside the lines of your reality, lies the possibility that your path can derail from a favorable course and that's where heartbreak exists. It exists within the mindset that if everything doesn't go exactly according to plan, , there is no happily ever after available to you.

The pain of fairytales comes in denying that somewhere along the way we lost grip of reality and believe our wants control our existence. Even as contrary information presents itself, we continue to believe magic will occur, our story will get back on track, and all will right itself in the end, as long as it stays within the confines of what we know.

Why do we do it? We do it because we all want to be happy and everyone knows that fairytales have happy endings. But, fairytales aren't solely to blame for our delusions just those that keep us believing we are owed a happy life and that some divine or magical force will grant it to us in the exact way we expect for it to happen. This becomes particularly ingrained in our thinking as we watch those around us achieve what appears to be a fairytale ending. Also, it is more pleasant to believe that you will meet the person of your dreams and live happily ever after, than it is to believe you will meet your hearts' desire who in 5-years could become dissatisfied, engage in an affair, divorce you, take the house, cat, car, and prefer never to hear from you again.

Fairytales offer a best-case scenario. After all, navigating your life waiting for disaster to strike would be a tragic existence, so we turn to a happy ending to keep us going, and use a strategically written story of romance where good triumphs evil as fuel.

Why is the happy ending so convincing? Fairytales use flowery words like "victory," "true love," and "destiny" and swirl them together with fantasy to implant a belief that we can achieve anything. It is true. We can do anything but in real life there are no magic wands to make things happen perfectly. You must take action, you must be willing to retool your thinking towards possibility, and even then "happily ever after" is not guaranteed. With knowledge that things do not just happen to you, it is important to remember that despite believing something is your destiny, logic tells us that simply wanting it to be true does not make it so.

For instance, let's say that most of the time we are rational people. I imagine you see yourself as realistic, and not completely delusional, so let's start there. Given this mindset, you understand all aspects of life do not go exactly according to your plan. Therefore, to compensate, you accept some level of disruption but consider those few hardships as manageable, right?

Yes. There will be infrequent surprises but who hasn't had to replace a light bulb?
Yes. There will be arguments with villainous characters but nothing from which you can't recover.
Yes. There will be an occasional scraped knee but thanks to Johnson & Johnson you are covered.

All of the above are minor disruptions that occur in day-to-day life. These are things that we anticipate so we prepare to rebound and, as such, our happily ever after proceeds direct to Oz. However, what happens to your fairytale when something unexpectedly radical happens to you? Do you have a hard time imagining the unimaginable or the "worst case scenario"? Are you able to stay hinged to your power to adjust and let your story do the same? Well, let's use the examples from above.

> What happens if not only your light bulbs burn out but you have an electrical fire and your house burns down?

> What happens if not only are you arguing with your partner but you separate or are considering divorce?

> What happens if not only are you hurt but now you are suffering?

A fairytale life assumes that you are armed and well-equipped to handle whatever may arise as long as it does not generate too much disruption and, immediately afterward, all aspects proceed as planned. The good news is, for the most part, that this is true.

Life is primarily a series of cause and effect events that are the result of choices we make and therefore our responses to each allow us to take the hit – good or bad – and move forward. The good and bad news is that life is unpredictable. It being unpredictable can be great and work for us in positive ways that surprise us and enrich our lives. The bad news? Surprises, especially unpleasant ones, can knock us flat.

These events can leave us dazed, and feeling hopeless about the possibility for our future. No matter how much we prepare or believe in our ability to master a scenario, sometimes surviving the unforeseen circumstances, for which we are ill-equipped and unprepared, make us question our value, our beliefs, and whether we can go on living. This is the double-edged-sword of fairytales. They make you believe that you can turn fiction into reality but when make-believe doesn't turn out as expected, you can feel forsaken and abandon all hope for happiness.

Ultimately, I believe that living happy should be your number one priority everyday even if things aren't going your way. Whatever that looks like for you, it is possible to integrate flexibility into the choices you make.

~

Being present in your life is one thing and having control over it is quite another. I'm not saying change who you are or you will never be happy. Not at all. I am pretty organized, structured, and believe living a regimented life keeps me sane. I am not suggesting that accepting chaos is the only way to be content. No way! In fact, I am one of those people who see a parent allowing their kid to run crazy in a restaurant and develop an eye twitch. I want to grab both parent and child, sit them in a corner and ask, "What the hell is wrong with you? Act normal."

No. I am not the authority on parenting. No. I do not believe that normal is actually "a thing." However, I am certain that unnecessary mayhem is not my bag.

I am a creature of habit and would explode without planning and living with organization. So if the idea of changing your 30+ year ingrained behavior is giving you heart palpitations, I understand. From one neurotic to another, I would like to tell you not to worry., and to know that this anxiety is part of you, but do you know it is not all of you?

I want to be clear about what this means. It means that above all I am advocating you accept that happily ever after will require work. It always did. Whether or not you will work is completely up to you. Bare minimum: consider that while right now life may feel like it's not been going according to plan that can be okay. I have a secret to tell you: it never was. There are things in this world we can know but there never was or will be a "life plan" that goes exactly as we want it to. I will help you to identify if you're living in a place of obsession over control and how to acknowledge those feelings to allow room for leniency.

There will be several truth bombs in this book. Some you may like. Some you may accept. Some you may have already thought of yourself. And some you may hate, reject, and know you would never fathom. Here's one for you; you have zero control over the outcome of every situation in your life. ZERO.

You can try your little toosh off to make things go your way and sometimes they will but guess what? A lot of the time, they won't. Life may never go according to plan and the sooner you make space for this thinking the sooner you will come to terms with what makes you unsatisfied with your current state of being.

We can take action everyday to design a reality that supports the overall structure we want for our lives. We can be accountable for how our thoughts affect our well-being. We can accept that sometimes being sad and devastated is just a part of the gig; while it sucks and hurts like hell, there is a way to use that pain to serve us, grow us, and make us stronger. To do all this, we will uncover why hanging on to your fairytale is important to you, what parts of your it are nonnegotiable and what parts aren't, what holds you back from moving-on and how to grieve so you can, and how to create a life that allows you to accept that sometimes shit goes wrong and there is nothing you can do about it.

I'm not trying to torture you. I want you to see there are places in your story that we can look that might help you find a way to tolerate your current state of being, to stop letting it control you, and instead use it to teach you.

Rerouting an idea you've had ingrained in your mind since childhood is not easy but it is doable. We are not children anymore and our experiences as a 30+ something far exceed those of a prepubescent child. Point is you've lived more now than you did when the fairytale was planted and you know better, even if you don't want to admit it. You do.

Case in point, thanks to Mom, Dad, and Grandma, as children we believed that not only are we liked by all things in this world, but that we should also be granted all the things we like. As adults, we've lived enough to know this is not true. We've been disappointed, heartbroken, and considered unlikable plenty to know that we are not everyone's cup of whiskey and this world is a crazy place. As a rebound, we recover by defining our rejections as not right for us and so we go in search of all the right stuff to get our ideal reality back on track.

Despite some adversity, we still don't abandon our happily ever after. Instead, we convince ourselves the circumstances weren't right and once we find the perfect people, places, and things, our happy ending will emerge. This is the right kind of thinking but if you don't accept that shit can go wrong - no matter how perfect your pronouns - then you'll continue to be disappointed. In which case, I ask you to consider this: even if all the right people, places, and things fell into your lap at exactly the right time and you were granted everything you wanted, do you think that disappointment and heartbreak will avoid you? That nothing bad, sad, or unfortunate will ever occur?

Realistically, we understand that a fairytale is a story. Regardless, we choose to believe a knight in shining armor will come save us and fulfill our heart's desires or that eventually, all pieces and parts of our story will align and all will be right in the end. Perhaps, today's fairytale is less fairy godmother with a glass slipper spell and more of an opportunity for us to see the magic we have within ourselves when shit gets hard. Either way, we take all elements, fact or fiction, and choose to believe what we want. We tell ourselves happiness is an all-or-nothing scenario. We become our own enemy by believing that if everything doesn't happen as planned then there can be no happy ending, and our life cannot have true satisfaction. Believing this is destructive to our well-being and leads us down a path of misery and despair.

Fairytales mean well. I believe they exist to encourage our dreams, challenge our ideals, and force us to see that we are capable of greatness. You are great and you should know that! If you don't, consider this your official stamp of approval. However, your story is not entirely the same as a fairytale.

The beauty of fairytale is that we can manipulate it however we want. We can control it and with ease, even bend the outcome permanently to our needs. Your story, however, is far less predictable and while malleable, often requires a great deal of effort and dedication towards its achievement. For these and other reasons, it is imperative that we become committed to who are, what we want, what we need and stand in integrity for that.

Life is a beautiful thing and, to be happy, it is necessary that we believe our own hype. However, a part of that beauty is choosing to see us as the same fabulous, wonderful, magical, and amazing humans even as our story changes and as life gets hard.

Hardship can be one of life's most permanent lessons for growth and prosperity. It challenges us to evolve and experience the unknown. It allows us to step outside consistency and see if we are capable of adapting to change. Change is not easy for everyone. Not everyone is comfortable leaping outside of his or her comfort zone to absorb the fear of unpredictability. However, the unknown is where possibility, progress, and some might say happiness lives. I believe happiness is available to each of us but we can only access it if we stop fighting the ebbs and flows of our story and adapt to the needs of our situation instead of expecting our situation to adapt to our needs.

If you're reading this, I think it's safe to say your road to "happily ever after" no longer follows the yellow brick kind. Sorry, Dorothy! A bit more bad news - there is no Oz!

If that was like taking a bullet, I apologize. Sincerely, I do, but someone had to tell you. Oz, much like a few of the disparaging things I'd be willing to bet you believe about yourself, is Not Real. Some good news: while there is no Oz, which should completely set your mind at ease and lower the beating you're giving to yourself about reality, there is you and all your amazing qualities to turn around what may seem like a dismal existence.

~

What is the truth? What you had expected for the life you imagined and your feelings about it have become your enemy.

Why? Because you have chosen to believe that you are everything other than the fabulous, wonderful, magical, and amazing human that you are!

How? The story you've bought into suggests you are anything other than a fabulous, wonderful, magical, and amazing human being, and currently, that bitch is running the show!

Look, our story is an ever-changing thing that, despite our growth in years, becomes a very solid part of us. If you had imagined your life playing out a certain way for as long as you can remember, well, consider those thoughts have been in there for a really long time. You've accepted them as real. They're no longer a "what if". They are a "when". And, because you've committed to this thinking, you have developed quite the attachment.

Just like getting out of any serious relationship, it is going to require time and effort to see things for how they are versus how you expected. Even worse, to see them how they are means accepting your life may never turnout that way. This doesn't mean you should burn your storybooks, lose hope, and abandon thoughts of a happy life. Let's not get dramatic!

You are allowed to still believe in magic, love, hope, and happy endings but, if you're here with me, then chances are there is a life-sized crater somewhere between who you are, what got you to this place, and where you want to be, telling you "YOU SUCK!" and it is standing in the way of you being happy. To get to it, you need to build a bridge of truth that will involve going in search of what is creating a roadblock. To move the block, you will need to put practices in place to get the obstructions out of the way. And to experience the breakthroughs that will permit you to deal with some of these serious feelings, you will need to be willing and dedicated to bridge this gap!

Hearing there is a roadblock in the way of your dreams can be life altering and hard. What's even harder? Knowing it. Going in search of it. Practicing It. Loving you through it. Accepting it.

There is a difference between hearing something and accepting it. Acceptance means you have come to terms with how it can and will affect your life. With this, you are prepared to move forward in a direction to find peace, happiness, fulfillment, and prosperity. Hearing something can mean you are aware of it but choose not to recognize its mental, emotional, and physical impact. Your refusal prevents you from receiving it and refusing to receive it affects your ability to see how it is affecting your future.

Hearing something and accepting it allows us to process how we feel and prepare our life for impact. This is where your happiness lives. Whereas, hearing something and not accepting it can be long, painful, and like the movie Groundhog Day, where avoidance creates a repetitive anguish you relive each time you remember it's there.

Hearing something and not accepting it means that while you have information, you reject it so your story never changes and there is no forward movement. This is where your pain lives. The unfortunate truth that exists in hearing and not accepting information is that wishing something into reality is not enough. Sometimes, avoiding this is the hardest roadblock of all.

I am in no way suggesting that feeling optimistic about your future is bad. Hells to the no! We need optimism to keep us going. In fact, being happy is my number one priority every day so there's no way I would tell you not to make it yours. I am of the opinion that if you're not happy with yourself then you can't positively contribute to life – yours or others. However, there is a fine line between ignorance and truth.

Being hopeful about something you know and refusing to accept it poses challenges that will take you nowhere fast. Besides, you can't get *over* emotional turmoil. You must go *through* it. You must process all feelings that come with it if you want to move on and find a way to be happy.

There is no good that comes from pretending you're fine when you're not. Neglecting what is does not change it. The more energy you spend pretending you're "OK" is counterproductive. Not only does denial introduce you to a whole new level of emotional challenges, which we'll discuss later, but, when it comes to achieving happiness, consciously trying to avoid something actually makes you hyper focused on it.

Think about it - have you ever noticed that when you try to ignore something it becomes more apparent? Let's take, for instance, a pimple. I'm obsessed with popping pimples. Not only will I search for my own to pop, but I'll search those bad-boys out on my husband too. He hates it. I love it. We survive.

A pimple, much like an emotional trauma is a part of you. It can hurt you, my pimples hurt me, and releasing it feels amazing! The roadblock you're experiencing now is just like a pimple that needs release. It is weighing on you, taking-up real estate in your life, going nowhere fast, and growing more and more painful each millisecond. God forbid anyone touches it or talks to you about it! You're sensitive to it and are not receptive of others pointing it out or discussing it. The downside, mental, emotional, and physical baggage are not capable of being extracted simply by popping a pimple. You won't find release by neglecting it anymore than you can by hoping it will just go away.

In our efforts to overcome life's obstacles, when we tell ourselves everything is going to be okay, we minimize our pain and, in doing so, neglect the value happiness holds in our life. Being okay is nonsense unless you want to live a mediocre life. You can't live happily being 'OK' and you shouldn't want to live an 'OK' life either. Blech – that makes me want to vomit! You should want to be better than okay! That's why focusing on the positive amidst a life crisis will not heal it. Sure. Focusing on the good is a great way to achieve positivity but, if you're unhappy, you need to know why before you can move forward feeling uppity about life.

As I said before, I am a proponent of making happiness a daily priority but I don't believe you can cure hurts by focusing on positivity instead of what is causing you pain. Sometimes, we need more than positive affirmations to heal our hurt. We need to get messy and lay down in the gutter with our pain, feel all its emotions, paint its fingernails, braid its hair, and understand where it's coming from in order to transform it into something that grows us. That mess is in you so no amount of wishful thinking or positive self-talk is going to make it evacuate the premises.

Why? Because, you can be a completely positive person who was dealt a rough hand and is living a very painful existence. It's possible. I know. I consider myself an optimistic person who was dealt a raw deal and who wound up living a very miserable life for a lot longer than I care to admit which I will share later in further detail. Point is healing will require you to become introspective with your entire self and demand you to do more than spout off a few positive affirmations to get you there.

I agree with the sentiment of personal development in that a positive mind creates a positive life. However, telling yourself you're fine, when you're not, is not helpful. If your life is in turmoil, no amount of telling yourself that you're the happiest you've ever been will make it so. We must deal with our garbage and take it out for disposal or else it will develop an odor and, quite possibly, fuck up the joint.

Ultimately, we cannot talk ourselves out of misery. We must go through it and feel as bad as required until we can find true healing. Lying to your heart and denying your emotions about what is will not empower you. In fact, your efforts to negate it shine a light on its existence and open you up to more disappointment. Subsequently, as time goes on, your battle of mind over matter can make your attempts to bury the presence of truth harder. As a result, it sucks the life from you, weighs you down, and begins to make you believe that happiness is unattainable.

Why? Again, we want what we want but truth is continual. It's alive; it is within you, affecting all aspects of you and it will not be silenced, no matter how hard you try to drown it out. Once you are alerted to it, it will go on no matter how you reject it because reality cannot be ignored and trying to do so will damage you, your soul, and all the ways that you exist right now and in the future.

We reject the truth in our lives out of fear. Fear of what it means, whom it makes us, and all of the unknowns. In denying our reality, we do so in an effort to clench the fantasy we invested in years ago. Holding on to something that eludes us does not make us crazy for doing so, but it does make us desperate, and that desperation can overshadow the parts of our well-being that crave healing and honesty.

In the process of holding on to the past, we miss our life. You are not wrong for wanting the life you want, but if you are sad, you are because you have defined so much of who you are by it. To acknowledge what is happening and all the ways it doesn't suit the life you had imagined does not mean you give-up on the idea of a happy life. It simply means you allow yourself to grieve all elements of how you thought it would play out. It does not mean you are killing your fairytale but it does mean that, in order to go on living a fruitful life, you need to mourn the loss of all pieces and parts of you affected by it.

~

I am a huge believer in setting our intentions and sending them out into the universe. I believe that in doing so we allow ourselves to become super clear about what it is we want and conveying that message outward helps us to receive it back. Notice I said, "helps". I did not say "guarantees".

The reason I caution focus on being okay versus being happy is because the universe is full of energy and sometimes denying our feelings and putting energy out there doesn't secure we'll receive what we want back. No sense in hoping for mediocrity when the outcome is already a crapshoot. Shoot for fantastic and if it comes back shit-tastic, well, then it's time to learn a lesson about fairytales. After all, you already know they're not real.

Hopefully, by now, you are painfully aware that "fairytales" are bullshit and yet, despite all rational thought and evidence to support this, you still expect someone to swoop-in and say you're wrong. I hate to disappoint you so early in our relationship but all relationships inevitably include some level of dissatisfaction and this book will include a lot of those same painful truths. Truths I learned along the way to acceptance and happiness. Therefore, in the spirit of setting an honest expectation up front, I will tell you you're right; fairytales are bullshit.

Welcome to the truth! Life is hard and, to be happy, it requires work. There are no fairy godmothers, magical wands, and no easy buttons. Thanks, Staples. Everyone has shit to deal with and, despite all that shit, the upside is that 'happily ever after' is available to anyone willing to work for it.

Based on whatever motivates your fairytale, generally, all of us would like our stories to end happy. If you're reading this, it's likely your current situation does not feel all that magical and your narrative has not played out the way you had expected. It's likely you're tired of feeling envious of those who seemingly live the life you want. It is okay. You can be mad. You can feel slighted. I did. I've been there. All is not lost.

Your "happily ever after" does not elude you. Switching up thoughts that give a play-by-play on how things should have turned out but didn't won't be easy, but it is totally doable. We will get down and dirty with feelings that convince you life sucks and go in search of all in your life that doesn't. Don't be afraid; I will teach you how to find your way back to the yellow-brick road, Dorothy.

~

At this juncture, you might not consider the way things are going as living, rather just existing. Living means that you feel actively involved in your life and despite having good and bad elements, you still believe in the possibility for a happy life. You believe that no matter what happens, fulfillment and happiness is available to you and no matter what does or doesn't transpire you can handle it.

Existing means that the only real involvement you have in your life is to achieve the happily ever after. It is an obsession. Everything you do, think, or feel, is laser focused on it. You are not creating space for possibility, because that would mean taking into consideration those good and bad things could happen to take you off course. You are only interested in the fairytale. You have a one track mind that says, "My life will have x-y-z and there are no options for an alternative." If you feel this way, it is important to understand that I cannot tell you what will make you happy, but I can tell you that I know what it is like to be under the weight of existing.

Facing our reality, and truth's that weigh on you like a 500lb pimple, is some heavy shit. To get out of your life slump it will require a willingness to be honest with you, a commitment to understand that you want to move forward, and a little mess. I'm talking ugly cry, boxes upon boxes of tissues, and looking at yourself while continually asking the question, "How did I get here?" more times than you can count.

The information contained herein will validate that something life altering has happened to you. No one has the power to invalidate your feelings as much as no one has the ability to heal them more than you.

Let's put all that on loudspeaker right now; you have the power to keep you in this place of despair and see your life as no more than the sum of your struggle. Or, you have the power to change the filter through which you are seeing your life and thereby also transform your story.

That said, this book will also confirm that 'happily ever after' *still* exists if you are willing to go in search of what it can look like and how to adjust to make it happen.

To find it, you need to get specific and realize your value in this life. We'll discuss how to do this.

To live it, you need to acknowledge that sometimes the map to a fairytale is a path less traveled. We'll find your direction.

Avoiding pain and refusing to acknowledge the severity of it will prevent you from accessing your joy. To pull you from a life-rut and identify how to get you to a place of acceptance, I will give you the option to grieve your perfect reality. I will help you see that the expectation to live "happily ever after", as well as how and when you had intended to do it, is what is keeping you sad. In short, I will help you to see that understanding your suffering is the key to happiness and part of that comes when you accept that there is no definition for 'happily ever after'. You must go in search of it.

The good news is you already have all the answers on how to do get your happy back, but we need to move something out of the way to get you to a place where you can be truthful with yourself about how you're seeing your story.

~

Hi. My name is Shannon and I am a recovering fairytale addict. I mostly get down with Tinkerbell but I totally bought into a fixed idea of "happily ever after". When I found out we were struggling with infertility, the idea of living in opposition to my family fantasy royally fucked me up for several painstaking years.

After 4 years of trying unsuccessfully to conceive, I found myself in a depression in which I contemplated my reason for living if I couldn't bare a child of my own. In year four of my depression, I was tired of being sad, hating my body, my existence, and life. From there, I was on a mission to crawl my way out of the shitty life I felt I was living and back into one that allowed me to feel genuinely happy.

As a means through which to understand my emotions, I started journaling. Before I knew it, I was writing a book about infertility. Specifically, a book about how infertility sucks, but you as a person do not. A book that addresses all the complicated feelings you may experience candidly. A book that addresses the depressive complex you can develop with your infertility struggles from someone who lives it too. A book that acknowledges your pain, hysteria, and suffering are not ridiculous or crazy. A book that is not written by a PhD or therapist but from someone who knows how it feels to be at war with themselves. A book that says everything you're feeling makes sense but you can't sustain a happy life holding onto the pain or keeping those feelings in. A book from someone who has found success in understanding that infertility and the depression it can bring are not your fault. Rather, your feelings are the result of grieving a fairytale life you had expected and you are not foolish for wanting it.

Let's put it out there flat: this book and its contents contain real life shit that happened as a result of our infertility. It will explore how infertility affected my husband, and me, my family, and, essentially, every aspect of my life. In it, I will share what tools I found useful navigating through it all.

Hopefully, you will find ways to move forward with infertility. You may not relate to some or all of my processes and you may even poo-poo some of my cheeky examples. That is more than OK. After all, not everyone can appreciate a good pun. Maybe, you don't like what I have to say or maybe you're not in a place where you're ready to hear it. Either way, aside from the movie quotes, song references, and one-liners intended to bring some levity to an otherwise intense topic, I hope that what you find is real, raw, sensitive, and a sense of belonging that shows I'm honored to share what worked for me with you.

~

In the process of outing our struggle with infertility and writing this book, I had a few naysayers advise that the title and my messaging was "too aggressive."

First, I acknowledge right here and now that I can be a bit too much. I often lovingly say that I am not everyone's cup of whiskey. That is the charm of me! Also, I don't drink tea. I don't even like the smell of tea, so while the reference does not personally land with me, if you prefer tea to whiskey to soften it up a bit, choose the metaphor you will. Regardless, I'm a little ironic, just like Alanis Morissette's *Jagged Little Pill*, that's both parts scary uncomfortable and good for you. You have to both swallow me whole and feel it burn all the way down or not at all. Whatever you choose, know that my intention is always good, even if the message packaged complete with black leather, skulls, diamonds, and hints of neon pink is not what you want.

Next, my response to the notion that the title is aggressive is, you're fucking right it is! Look, if you don't like my messaging, you're sure as shit not going to like my title. It's kind of a two part deal; if you don't like how the writer talks, then you're probably not going to like how they write, name shit, reference things, or title them. I could go on for days about why I feel completely empowered and validated by the title of this book but, for now, I'll simply say yes, you are correct. You're damn right the title of this book is aggressive because struggling with infertility is some rough stuff.

Infertility is not like getting the flu, or a scratchy throat, or even that 500lb pimple we talked about earlier that you swear has its own heartbeat. It's not something you can just get rid of or heal. In some instances like ours, which I will dive into later, you never fully heal. You make a choice about how you want to see your life and move forward knowing that there will always be good days, bad days, and days where you feel sort of "in between." That can mean you have children or that you don't. Either way, the experience of infertility never "leaves you" and, as such, you might say it is a desperate situation that deserves drastic attention for all involved.

Infertility overshadows all aspects of a person's life and, because of this, I felt the need to be crystal clear in asserting my message as succinctly as possible. This disease fucking sucks and, if you let it, it can control your whole life through the lens of suffering. It's not a willing decision to let feelings of helplessness, depression, or defeat takeover. Let's get clear on that right now. It just happens. The willingness comes when we realize what is happening and how gravely our circumstances impact our life and we allow them to stick around. From there, we are presented with a choice to move on or stay put in our grief.

My answer is, yes. Infertility is really fucking aggressive, and because of that the messaging is aggressive, and because of that the title needs to be simple, short, and impactful in communicating that, while this situation is so completely sucky, you are not. Again, all said with peace and love, with the flavor of a *Jagged Little Pill*. Thanks, Alanis! You're the best!

So, here we are, ready to dive-in and discover what in the hell is going on with you that's making you feel like you suck? To do this, let's do a mental cleansing.

You are not perfect. I am not perfect. No one is perfect. No one has a perfect life and no one expects your life to be perfect. Relinquish that to the universe. Expel it and get it out because the longer you hold on to the idea that you're fucked-up the longer you're going to feel fucked up. It's not a matter of calculating all your imperfections and submitting them to the "Universe" and cashing-in on who gets the award for most tragic. I know it might sound crazy but if you spend more time tallying the things that aren't going right than focusing on who you are, the value you bring to this world, and all the good there is still left to accomplish, the more you're going to feel like you're failing this thing called life.

Real life shit happened to you, it happened to me, and fucked us up. Woo – getting that out feels good and I'm not ashamed to admit it! It is my hope that you too will get to a place where you are not ashamed to admit how all of this has made you feel. After all, that is the basic premise for the book: how I can help you feel less fucked up and happier. See how we're already connecting the dots?

CHAPTER 3:
SHIT HAPPENS

L et's get honest. This book will not tell you how to get pregnant. This book is not about you getting pregnant.

What in the hell is this book about? This is about you. It is not about your future baby. Honestly, I'm indifferent about you having a baby at all. Pause for, "Fuck her", reaction.

If continuing to try to have a baby is a requirement for your happiness, then go get it! However, I'm more concerned with how you will you survive if you can't have a child and how you can reconnect to your value of self.

I'm not trying to be "Debbie Downer. I'm the opposite, actually. I want you to feel like you already win at life baby or no baby, because you do.

Remember, I already believe that you are fabulous, wonderful, magical, and amazing. I do believe in having hope and trying until we can't try anymore. However, in terms of infertility, the health and happiness of you and your relationship must come before the baby, or you and it won't survive. If me saying so is a turn off, here are more un-arousing topics we'll explore.

Will you find happiness if you never conceive?

———

How will you survive infertility mentally, emotionally, and physically?

How is infertility affecting your relationships?

Where does your value develop if your focus is always on having a baby?

Are you choosing to believe a story that suggests "happily ever after" is unavailable to you?

I'm not a hater of men and women who struggle with infertility and want to maintain faith they will get pregnant. If you're committed to becoming parents, then continue with that focus. Go on with your bad self! I was that woman. I struggled for years to achieve my "happily ever after": husband, 3 kids, 2 dogs, 1 cat, 2 cars, a house that had a wrap-around porch with a swing, and a white picket fence. Again, I will share more about my struggle with you later but the point is I want you to do what you want to do but I want you to consider that striving for something you don't have, and maybe never will, does not make you incomplete.

Having a baby didn't work for us but it wasn't for a lack of trying and with each failed pregnancy I devalued myself. I want to help you *not* do the same.

What happened as a result of me defining myself by our inability to get pregnant? I fell apart.

I was unprepared for the mental, emotional, and physical damage of infertility. Not only the harm it caused me but everything in my life. It changed who I was and it fucked my shit up hard. For as much as this book is about you, it is also about me, and sharing my journey in hopes you don't fall down the same rabbit hole.

In the words of Sarah Knight, author of *Get your Shit Together*, "I lost my shit so you don't have to." You're welcome.

CHAPTER 4:
THE DIAGNOSIS

I was 29 years old when Scott and I got married. On our wedding night, we had intentional unprotected sex for the first time. I remember thinking that allowing my husband to ejaculate inside me for the first time felt ceremonial and intimidating, because it felt like at that exact moment we were making a baby.

The action of allowing someone to climax inside me was so foreign, scary, and beautiful that when I felt him do it, my entire body became tense. I was tense because there was no going back. There was no changing the fact that he had done the very thing I had lived in fear of someone doing for 29 years. He and I had done the thing that makes babies and for some reason I felt a little bit like I was in trouble and also like I had never been closer to any human in my whole life.

I'm pretty sure it was the first time I had ever had sex and wanted to cry at the same time. I wasn't emotional because I was sad or scared. I was emotional because that moment was and would be the beginning of several moments that would change my life. My awareness around fear, sexuality, love, and attachment to everything that was happening in those few seconds of intercourse was so intense.

After it was over, I remember lying next to him, naked, in bed. His skin touching mine felt nonexistent. It felt like we were one person. It felt like we had done the biggest thing we had ever done together, immediately, after doing an already huge thing like get married. It was a lot to take in but in a way that felt amazing. He was my husband now and I was his wife and in that moment, in that hotel room, we made one of many decisions together that would change our life.

6 months into our marriage, nothing was happening. I was still dealing with periods and no baby, and for some reason, I had an unshakable feeling something was wrong. Call it a guttural reaction. Call it woman's intuition. Call it "Shannon is impatient". Call it whatever you want. After 6 months of unprotected sex, I wasn't pregnant and I decided that was long enough, but also time o see an infertility specialist.

I found my infertility specialist online searching through the "approved" and "in-network" infertility specialist list on our healthcare provider's website. I had no idea what I was looking for. I had no idea what infertility really was. I had no idea what I was doing. Ultimately, I chose someone who was close to home, covered under health insurance, and in his provider biography listed something close to, "I help women conceive." He was close, he was covered, and he gets women pregnant – we had a winner!

The first time I went to see the man who I decided was going to get me pregnant, I remember feeling lost, confused, but also understood for the first time. Within minutes of talking through my history with endometriosis and polycystic ovaries, coupled with frequent urination, constipation, and insanely difficult periods, he explained that I had just described to him a series of symptoms that women who struggle with infertility often experience.

It was at that time that we would decide to engage in laparoscopic surgery to firmly deduce whether or not I was suffering from endometriosis and perhaps, others symptoms relating to infertility. It was at that time that we would decide to stop guessing at what could be the issue, and make a big decision to pursue surgery to understand what was going on. As I mentioned, I am a woman of action. I was tired of waiting. Good or bad, I wanted results.

What came next was a lot of humbling news; from the laparoscopic surgery we learned that I struggle with stage IV endometriosis and polycystic ovaries. What does that mean?

According to Endometriosis Foundation of America, "Endometriosis occurs when tissue similar to the lining of the uterus (endometrium), is found in regions outside of the uterus, in other words, where the tissue should not be. It affects around one in every ten women and is mostly unrecognizable, misdiagnosed, and mistreated."

According to American Society of Reproductive Medicine (ARMS), there are four stages of endometriosis. Stage I is stated to be minimal, II is mild, III is moderate, and IV is severe. By stage IV, the disease has spread to other organs in the pelvic region as well as the ovaries. This stage of the disease can impact an individual's anatomy, cause severe pain, infertility, and scar tissue that can bind organs or tissue together, this is also known as adhesions.

Polycystic ovary syndrome or PCOS is a female hormonal disorder. According to American Society of Reproductive Medicine (ARMS), polycystic ovary syndrome is a common hormone disorder that affects 5%-10% of women. Like all syndromes, PCOS is a collection of problems that are found together. Not all women with PCOS have all the same symptoms. To be diagnosed with PCOS, a woman must have 2 of 3 possible issues: chronic lack of ovulation (anovulation), chronic high testosterone (hormone) levels (hyperandrogenism), and ovaries that have multiple small cysts containing eggs (polycystic).

According to the Mayo Clinic, there are 3 signs or symptoms of PCOS. These include irregular periods, where menses may not come each month or the period cycle is inconsistent, increased levels of male hormones (i.e. testosterone) where excess facial or body hair and acne may occur, as well as polycystic ovaries which could cause ovaries to become swollen or enlarged, and contain cysts.

I wasn't shocked to learn that something crazy was going on inside me. I wasn't shocked because since my first period, menstruation has been a living hell. Every period since I can remember has been a battle.

In my menstrual dictionary, "period cramps" does not begin to define the level of pain endured. Needless to say, there is no flow to my "flow" and I've never had a great relationship with the uterus taking up real estate in my internal cavity.

To offer insight into the level of cramping, imagine a baby Velociraptor using its talons to gouge you and tunnel through your skin or a wild bull possessed by the devil seeing red and going buck wild. It's pretty awesome – said with layers of sarcasm.

For years, I mostly ignored the pain assuming it was "normal" and I will touch on this more later, but, feeling helpless, I paid it little attention until our infertility diagnosis. Infertility shined a light on the damage endometriosis and polycystic ovaries had on me. However, I wasn't prepared for feeling that level of truth.

The truth is, whatever your infertility diagnosis stems from, it brings pain.

My husband and I share this struggle but, for a long time, I felt it was all mine. It was happening in my body but it was happening to him too. Admittedly, I didn't do a very good job at owning that, which I will also share more on later. I thought it was solely my struggle but he is my ride or die homie so, while I was down-and-out, he held it down in our marriage and I couldn't love him more for that. Ultimately, instead of dealing with the fact that endometriosis and polycystic ovaries was causing us to struggle with fertility, I found comfort in denial.

CHAPTER 5:
WHEN NO ONE CALLS
A SPADE A SPADE.

In my 20+ years of professional experience, I have had many mentors, some great and some not so great. During that time I have learned a lot about communication and how to be clear that all parties are walking away from the conversation with the same understanding about what is being communicated, or next steps, if there are any.

One of the most succinctly eloquent things I have learned in all those years is from a boss who loved to use the phrase, "say the words".

The first time I heard her say it I felt something in my brain switch on. It was like she got inside my head and empowered me to speak what was on my mind in a way that is flat. I love it so much, that you will find I refer to it in further detail later on, but it's because while the message is brief, it is powerful.

To me, "say the words" conveys so much. To me it says that it is far greater to set the expectation, than to not, so speak on it clearly, with intention, and so that both parties understand. I like this because it makes sense to me.

I'm a straight shooter. I like hearing the details quick and simple. I like knowing where I stand, who likes me, who doesn't, and I am generally happy to hear all of it. Truth. No one *likes* to hear they're not liked, but I'd rather know than live in the land of ambiguity. I guess that's just the Type-A in me.

After my surgery, something happened. My Type A persona split. I went from being the gal that wanted to have everyone give it to her straight and know all the details, to one that felt our doctor knew best.

I went from wanting to know how everything was going to play out, when, and who was going to participate, to believing our doctors when they told us that "you will" or "should be able" to get pregnant. I didn't have any further questions or concerns outside of that.

I believed that if they knew it *should* or *would* work, then the details didn't matter. Nothing about it was clear, quick, or simple and for some reason I became okay with that.

Honestly, I think I was glad to hear the *should* and *would,* because to be me it was better than the *can't* or the *won't.* I became glad to live in ambiguity because healing from the removal of adhesions during the laparoscopic surgery was no joke. Discovering that it would require more effort, money, and time our part to conceive was scary. Feeling confused, alone, and like an alien with Endometriosis and PCOS in my own body was a lot to process. I was overwhelmed and so I decided that I didn't need to know all the details, that was for the M.D. to figure out.

I found comfort and reassurance in the *should* and *would*. I found strength and possibility that we had the "all clear" and the next stop on our journey would be discovering that we were expecting. I took it all as positive and as certainty. I absorbed all of it as fact.

In my mind, *should* and *would* meant we were on our way to baby! As a result, I found myself saying things like, "we don't know what the problem is", to other people. I found myself thinking that the hard part was over..

Yet, we knew the problem! We knew that I was dealing with symptoms related to infertility and it was a possibility that with each period thereafter, the endometriosis could grow back. However, we "will" and we "should" get pregnant at any time became my focus.

I trusted my doctor. After all, he confirmed what I knew to be true for years; that there was some crazy shit going on inside my uterus that wasn't right. I believed that he and science held the answer and because I did, I also convinced myself that they would have the cure.

There's a part of me that wants to tell doctors all over the world to stop telling people struggling with fertility that "they will" or "they should" be able to get pregnant, but that would be unrealistic. It would be unfair. It would be me telling them to take the hope and faith and positivity away from people who so badly need it, so I will own my part in choosing to believe we would get pregnant. I will also own that part of that stemmed from years of pain.

I wanted to have faith that there would be an upside to what felt like torture. I wanted something to make all of it worthwhile. I couldn't accept how years of struggling with severe pain and thinking that it would all be worth it was for not. So, I rejected infertility, I believed in science, and I clung to hope that maybe sometimes it's okay not to call a spade a spade.

Again, hope, is not a useless emotion. I see the absolute need for it in any struggle, especially, infertility. It is powerful but I used it to deflect everything else that was going on and used denial to refuse to acknowledge it.

I don't blame my doctors for giving me hope. I don't even blame them for continuing to encourage it. I was there seeing them for a very specific reason; I wanted to get pregnant. I get that the hope needs to be shared by them as much as it does by me because that is what I'm essentially hiring them to do. However, there needs to be room for truth in hope.

There needs to be room for transparency not just in the good news, but also in the bleak. I know that not everyone is like me and wants people to "say the words" but I do believe there is a gap in the infertility space that needs to be addressed. There is a gap that needs to acknowledge the truth and that calling a spade a spade is very necessary.

I accept responsibility for how I was managing my feelings or better yet, not managing them, but I do wish that my doctors would have explained to me the statistics for a successful pregnancy for a woman who struggles with both Endometriosis and Polycystic ovaries. I understand that miracles happen everyday. I spent everyday thinking that some drug or ovulation schedule was going to my miracle that it was going to work because my doctor had seen "positive results in a majority of patients who struggle with similar symptoms". What I have learned is that what works for one doesn't work for all and because of my inability to see anything but hope I wasn't allowing in truth. The truth that it *may not happen* for us, and the reason I wasn't allowing that in was because it hurt.

The truth that we may never have a baby, despite all our efforts, was like taking a bullet. It blew my hope wide-open and made room for doubt.

The truth that gave me an awareness that my 'happily ever after' may not play-out how I had planned. I wasn't willing to make space for that.

~

What happened next, on our road to baby, is that I became obsessed with it. It caused me to live the next 4-years in a fog of denial, hurt, disillusion, and a big honking infertility depression. Oh, and I totally didn't give a shit about anyone or anything else in the process... including myself.

I was laser focused on a goal to have a baby. All other things would have to figure themselves out. Honestly, in my mind, there was very little time for anything else. Between daily doctors' visits, timed sexual encounters, and body temperature readings it was very mentally, emotionally, and physically time consuming. Nothing got in the way of my goals.

You know how people say, "Being married is a full time job?" Well, so is getting pregnant while struggling with infertility. I needed to split my attention between that and the full-time job that was paying for me to have a baby. It was inevitable that something was going to suffer but I was bound and determined that it would not be the pregnancy process.

Sadly, I admit that the thing I abandoned was my partner. I abandoned my husband and his pain, because I was too consumed with doing everything I needed to do to "prime my body" for a baby, while also feeling slighted in my frustrations. I will expand upon this in more detail later because it is my personal opinion that our relationship to self and our partners is very important not just with infertility but in life. However, I'm very lucky to have a partner who knew I was going through something bigger than me. Yet, he stuck by my side.

He never left me. He never shamed me or made me feel guilty. He never pushed me in an unsafe direction. He was patient and loving and exactly what I needed. I wish I could have been more of that for him.

Hindsight is 20/20 and, while navigating infertility was unchartered territory for us both, my hub is pretty gangster. I will reference him and our relationship much more throughout the book. Note: I use the word gangster to mean awesome because gangster is more fun than awesome.

You will notice that I frequently use personal reference to share the hardships I faced with infertility, as well as the struggles my husband faced, and how it can affect all relationships. I will talk about my family because, if infertility teaches us anything, it's how to define family. I will share what I did that kept me in a depression for 4-years and numb to my life. I will talk to you the way I talk to my family and friends, which means I will use sarcasm, cynicism, humor and profanity.

I can't tell you the number of times I will use words lke shit, hell, goddamn, fuck, or motherfucker but I'm sure a witty reader will give me the heads-up. Future thanks for that by the way. I will use movie and song references and jest to keep a life vibe flowing through the hard shit. I will tell you right away I am not a licensed therapist or PhD. I am a Life Coach, writer, and an Infertility Survivor. I am a person who lived through this, continues to live with it, and someone who has learned quite a bit about herself through it.

I am not an expert in anything but my life experiences, and me and even that is putting it loosely. Don't believe me? Just ask the voices in my head. Ultimately, I am not an expert in infertility. I will never, ever, Ever, claim to be that. I am just a girl that lives with infertility. I am someone who knows how difficult it can be to adapt and live with this disease. I am someone who refused to accept this as a "human condition" and is willing to share those experiences with you.

I am a person who wants to start a dialogue about how those who struggle with infertility feel. I want to give a voice to those who are lost. I want you to know that true happiness is still possible. I want you to hear that feeling sexy, sexual, and having good sex in your marriage is still out there. Sorry, Mom and Dad.

I wrote this because I believe a conversation needs to begin for those looking at infertility with all the same questions I had after 4-years and failing to conceive, "Now What?", "Why is this happening to me?", "What did I do wrong?", "Will I ever feel happy again?" and "Will life always just be ½ as good as it could have been?"

There is life and genuine laughter beyond your diagnosis. After all, you are more than just a vessel intended for the productivity of humans. Think about that. Your life's whole purpose is as a baby maker, really? If that were true, I'm pretty sure sex would feel more like work and a lot less fun. Again, sorry, Mom and Dad.

You are not worthless if you cannot get pregnant and "freak" is not an acceptable label for people who can't or don't have children. The number one thing Mom and Dad taught me was to be nice to others. It took me a few years of terrorizing my forever-patient older brother to latch on to that. Don't believe me? Just ask him how many times I "brushed" his hair with the wrong side of a brush. The number two thing they taught me was to be nice to myself. Infertility made me abandon #2. Yet again, sorry, Mom and Dad. I lost my way but, because of the two of you, I have found my way back. I love you.

You have value and if you cannot see it now I will help you find it. If you're struggling with your diagnosis, know you still have a purpose and an exciting life begging to be lived. You are worthy of an amazing existence. You are sexy, funny, intelligent, and lovable and have a great ass. If currently you lack self-confidence, it's okay to feel down on yourself but it is not okay to stay down. We will get you through this because you are fabulous, wonderful, magical, and amazing.

Before we get started, first, I want to say thank you for sharing your journey with me. I see you. I hear you. You're not alone.

Second, this will be hard. I'm talking getting gum out of your hair before you ultimately decide to cut it out because peanut butter doesn't work hard. Don't give-up.

Lastly, thank you for being brave and choosing to believe there is more to you than shooting sperm and or babies out of your body. Thank you for reading and, while I may not know you personally, we are already connected and my heart is already with you.

This is the type of experience that connects people and, while it is difficult and hard, it is manageable. You will get through this. I am here for you and I am glad we found each other. I already love you.

Take a breath. Let's begin.

CHAPTER 6:
YOU DO NOT SUCK.
INFERTILITY
DEFINITELY DOES!

T he "healing" side of me wants to come out the gate with something cheeky like, "Welcome, to your infertility!" Then, some game show music would ensue and a host (because that's ironic) would pop-out of nowhere with one of those long microphones from the 70's in a suit that looks like he just stepped-out of Goodfellas, and says, "You have Infertility? Get outta here!" Hell, we could even say it is Joe Pesci!

I WOULD start diving into the hard shit of this book that way because I want you to see there is light at the end of this tunnel.

I WOULD start it that way because there is an irony to this that you may not be able to see now.

I WOULD start it that way because I want you to know this will end with me telling you that to survive this you NEED to find a way to fall madly in love with yourself and have a giggle again. It IS possible and I will share with you how I learned to do that.

I WOULD do all these things but... okay, I just did.

Point is we're about to enter another dimension: a dimension that only a few understand and are not privileged to. No. This is not *The Twilight Zone*. This is infertility. Don't get me wrong; I wish I had Rod Sterling to tell me this episode of my life would be followed by a brief commercial break and then *confirm* it was a nightmare, but that will not happen.

What will happen and what happened to me was messy, scary, depressing, debilitating, enlightening, lonely, and rehabilitating. No, the pain and healing didn't occur all at the same time. It was more like an up and down sequence that went back and forth and occurred over time. No. This is not an "After School Special" anymore than it is an eerie episode of *The Twilight Zone*. The cold hard reality is, if you're struggling with infertility, it will be hard and for a while hard will define your life.

Whether you've been recently diagnosed or have been struggling with infertility for some time, here is the most important thing I can tell you: there is no way around it. There is only a way through it. Unfortunately, getting through will be less like Chutes and Ladders and more like running around Jurassic Park while being chased by a T-Rex. I'd like to offer you a "don't worry" but the truth is you will get hurt and your feelings will be a mess.

~

To get through this, you'll need to be furiously focused on deciding who you are now because the future is not the answer to your present. You are the answer to your present and what your future looks like is contingent on the steps you take now to be relentless in the pursuit of your happiness.

The facts are specific to your type of infertility and, in this book, we're **not** going to focus on what kind of infertility you have as much as we are focused on helping you emotionally heal from it. So we're going to "put baby in a corner" for a second and consider 2 types of infertility.

In corner 1, are those who have been unsuccessful at getting pregnant while having unprotected sex for more than 1-year.

In corner 2, are those who have been pregnant but are unable to carry a baby to term.

According to the CDC, about 6% of women in the U.S. ages 15-44 are unable to get pregnant after unprotected sex and about 12% of women in the U.S. are unable to carry a baby to term. I'm no mathematician but that means if you know 20 women between the ages of 15-44, given the 6% ratio, potentially 1 of those 20 will struggle with this issue.

Makes you kinda pissed to be that 1, right? Don't feel ashamed to say yes. I'm pissed about it too but there's nothing you or I can do about it. You want to hit someone, kick puppies, and kittens. You want to tell every single person that tells you, "Relax. It will happen when you relax" to shut-the-fuck-up! You potentially want to blame your vagina for every problem you've ever encountered in life and call your parents to say, "Thanks a lot for skimping on the fertility genes, guys. You really shit the bed and ruined my life." And, to top it all off, you want to scream, "Fuck you, Baby!" at every short person you see. I get it. I truthfully, painfully, and honestly do.

If I could reach-out and hug you through your pain, I'd be on you like white on rice but I can't. And you can't go blaming the universe, random short people, nor your vagina or your parents for the issues you face with infertility. Mostly, because that would be inappropriate but also because it wouldn't be right and it wouldn't change anything.

Like I said before, you cannot go around your feelings and survive infertility. Unfortunately, you're going to have to go through the scary, depressing, debilitating, enlightening, lonely, and rehabilitating pain to survive and we'll get into the nitty-gritty of how to handle thoughts on "why is this happening to me" in stage two but first let's deal with what does this mean for you now.

I have infertility. Now what? Considering our 20 to 1 example that also means there may not be someone you know directly (or who even knows themselves) struggling with infertility but, according to the "7 degrees of Kevin Bacon", a friend of a friend of a friend definitely knows someone that you know who is facing or will face this struggle. The point is, while it is completely shitty and you wouldn't wish it on your worst enemy, you may be one of few in your circle but you're definitely not alone.

Getting through this is going to be about putting in the work so put on some Marvin Gaye because it's time to Get It On!

Before we take a deep dive, I want to caution you to expect the following on your infertility journey:
Denial and Shock
Shock and Anger
Anger and Bargaining
Bargaining and Depression
Depression and Acceptance

You may recognize these as stages of grief. If you do, then you've hit the nail on the head. 20-life points for you!

Struggling with infertility has a lot of grief, crying, self-hatred, blame, confusion, alienation, pain, and recovery involved. You may also recognize that each stage contains the last one and that is intentional.

Your healing is like a teeter-tatter or a seesaw; just as you feel you've made it to your next stage you may find yourself dealing with a setback and right back to where you started. There is no shame in taking a few steps forward and a few steps back, consider that your process and a calling to pay attention to where you are on your journey for possible breakthroughs. So, get in the gutter with what is holding you back, and release your commitment to it to move forward.

CHAPTER 7:
DENIAL IS NOT JUST
A RIVER IN EGYPT.

At 15, I passed out in school from a painful period and was diagnosed with Mittelschmerz which is when you have pain associated with ovulation. At 17, I took so many Midol pills to dull the period pain that I vomited for an entire day. At 19, I was erroneously diagnosed with cancer. At 21, I saw a doctor for bowel dysfunction and frequent urination. At 23, I was misdiagnosed with IBS. At 29, I had a laparoscopy to investigate infertility and pain.

For most of my life, I have been affected by symptoms related to Endometriosis and PCOS and, at 29, I learned that most, if not all, previous diagnosis were wrong. While I did find some comfort in knowing there were less "things" wrong with me, that ease quickly faded when I realized suffering from infertility meant there was a strong possibility we would never conceive. The worst part of all, it would be my fault.

The laparoscopy unveiled I was suffering from symptoms related to infertility, stage 4 Rectovaginal Endometriosis and Polycystic Ovaries (PCOS). During the surgery, doctor's also discovered a benign tumor inside my uterus which would require a D & C procedure. For the next 4-years, my husband and I would engage in the most difficult journey of our lives, both individually and together.

Following our infertility diagnosis, my husband and I began a 4-year cycle of trying everything we could afford to get pregnant. This led to several rounds of IUI, Fertility Drugs, Acupuncture, depression, hair loss, weight loss, skin discoloration, and self-deprecating thoughts but no baby. On our journey to "baby", I lost myself and it wasn't until I started to question the value in living that I could see just how far down the rabbit hole I had gone. In a moment of questioning your life, your legacy, and the value you bring to this world, you become worn down by feelings of sadness and grief.

~

I was having dinner with my parents at our favorite restaurant in Pittsburgh. It was right in the middle of my silent battle with severe depressive thoughts. My husband, who is a born entrepreneur, was out that night working so my parents invited me to have dinner with them. This wasn't an odd occurrence; in fact, it was something that we had done quite frequently at this exact restaurant, and almost every weekend.

It was summer, my favorite time of the year. It was just the three of us, which is odd because I come from a family of 5, but I remember thinking it was nice to have an opportunity to talk with my parents one on one. I was engaged and as relaxed as I could be, and I was happy to be with them. In fact, being with my parents is one of my favorite things to do. They are great people, so just being in their presence makes you feel good and filled with love, but tonight that love was almost too much to take.

A typical night at dinner involves a few drinks, excellent food, and a lot of laughs. This particular night, I desperately wanted to laugh, but all I could feel was the shame, anger, and confusion of yet another month doped-up on hormones that resulted in a failed pregnancy. Somewhere between a glass of Malbec and my favorite salad, I started to think about how much I love my parents and how much I know they love me, and that if I couldn't have a child, then that must've meant I was unworthy to this kind of love; the sacred, ooey-gooey, and all encompassing kind that exists between a parent and a child.

Sitting there, laughing with them, and being present felt good, but at the same time the hurt was palpable. It was swirling in my head, looming in my heart, and sitting in that space in the back of your throat that feels like it's almost holding the tears in. The stronger the emotions, the more I tried not to talk, but then, just as Mother's do, mine gave me that inquisitive look. That look that makes you feel like they're peering into your soul and they know something is up. That's when she said, "What's wrong? Are you OK?" I remember taking a deep breath. The kind of breath that makes you feel like a balloon that finally gets to deflate and that's when I broke down crying into my osso bucco.

~

Situations like these weren't constant, and they did repeat themselves, but they brought no baby. Despite suffering from serious emotional turmoil, and insatiable urge to checkout of life, I knew I wasn't ready to give-up on me.

I knew that I wanted more for my life than crying into plates of food over casual conversation. I knew that I needed to take action for the kind of life that I wanted to live versus the one in which I existed, and that's when I decided to fight back. That's when I decided to fight for my life, my happiness, and feeling like I deserved those things with or without a child. That's when I decided I would make it my mission to stop identifying as infertile and understand that it is not me.

I did some research. I sought out varying perspectives, both western and eastern, and what I learned was infertility is a disease. I didn't ask for it and I didn't contract it. It is in me but it is not me. Learning this changed my life, my perspective, and who I was. Learning this helped me understand it is possible to come back from feeling like your life sucks and realize Infertility Sucks, You Don't... all you have to do is try!

If any part of this resonates with you, I hope it gives you the same sense of understanding it brought me. What I mean is when I sat down and really looked at the trajectory of my past to my infertile present I saw a path. I understand no one could have predicted endometriosis and PCOS would ultimately make me infertile because my Gram, Mom, and Aunt, have Endo and babies but – and I say this BUT with volume – someone should have explained to me what it *could* mean.

Yes. I understand as humans we err on the side of caution. I also know that some ultra conservatives would urge that telling women who struggle with painful periods associated with endometriosis and PCOS is reckless for fear they'd be wrong but I say, leave the ultra conservatives with their "sunshine and roses" vigilance and allow the rest of us to decide for ourselves. To me, the fact that no one ever mentioned there could be a problem and conception could be more than challenging is FUCKED!

Whew! Sometimes, you just need to say fuck.

What does this mean for you? Well, our future is undoubtedly affected by our past. There is no way anyone could have told me with any certainty that I would not be able to get pregnant. I know you're thinking, "What!? Just a few seconds ago, she said someone should have told her?" Right. I think they should have but I also understand why they didn't.

They didn't tell me that I was going to struggle with infertility but they didn't tell me that I could either and that lack of consideration, the lack of preparation I was robbed of, that's what makes me mad. I'm a planner. I like to know what could happen even if there is no guarantee. Preparation is key to me and the fact that, to this day, no one can tell me I won't be able to have a baby is mind-boggling but that's the charm of infertility. I have the eggs... regular periods... yadda-yadda... fact still remains, I have sex and there is no baby. So for you, it is important to understand this very key element: it is extremely unlikely that ANYONE could have predicted this for you... EVEN YOU. Denying what plagues us will almost certainly keep you stuck in your grief as much as avoiding that it is happening will.

Tough love: The charm of infertility is also the charm of life. Nothing is guaranteed.

If you suffer from infertility symptoms, not even discovering there is a likelihood that you may or may not get pregnant is enough to make this situation any easier. However, despite all the ambiguity of life, you are not born to live for a certain number of years, have a baby, raise "said baby", and then die. This is not your sole purpose, anymore than it is that of "said baby's" to repeat this cycle and provide you with grandchildren. That is not your lot in life. This is not anyone's lot in life.

You are expected to live. It is expected that your life will have purpose and meaning. Just as a baby does not fix a broken marriage, it will not fix a broken "ideal" life. Repeat after me, babies are not Band-Aids to any of life's problems. No Baby Band-Aids! You have to be sound and secure in your own image before you can give of yourself to anyone. Simply put, a baby does not give you purpose. Its presence can add meaning to your life but birthing humans does not define you. You are not merely a vessel that gets fucked, eats, and produces babies. I feel the need to say this to you with intensity for you to see how you are defining yourself: You are more than a fuckable, eating, vessel. Therefore, giving birth does not define you.

So what does this mean for your present?
This is a tough one because it brings-up questions like:

>What is your purpose if you cannot bear a child?
>Are you less of a man or woman if you cannot have a baby?
>Does not having a baby make you less effeminate or desirable?
>How are you contributing to your legacy if you don't produce a human?
>What does this diagnosis make you feel about yourself - if you're the infertile?
>What does this diagnosis make you feel about your partner - if they're the infertile?
>How do you feel about each other now – if you're the infertile and they're not or vice versa?
>Are you both communicating your feelings about this situation to each other?
>Can you move on together considering a possibility that there may never be a baby - and, I mean EVER?

These and other important questions can be used to help you move forward and process your feelings about where you are with infertility.

Here's a look at how the answers to those questions might look.

What is your purpose if you cannot bear a child? Me. I am my purpose; finding love within me and spreading it as often as possible keeps me connected to myself, and the beauty that can exist in this life. When I am in a place where I am having a hard time finding and feeling love, then I know I am out of alignment with my purpose and attention needs to be paid introspectively.

Are you less of a man or woman if you cannot have a baby? Despite what my hurt and anger let swirl around in my brain, the answer is no. Factually, I am no less of a woman if I cannot have a baby.

Does not having a baby make you less effeminate or desirable? The cold hard truth is I do feel less effeminate because I cannot bare a child, but dwelling on this takes me out of alignment with my love purpose. When I am out of alignment with my purpose is when I let the negativity creep into my brain and that is when the depressive thoughts takeover and I start to beat myself down.

How are you contributing to your legacy if you don't produce a human? I am contributing to my legacy everyday just by being alive. Whether I look at my life as if it has no value and I am worthless or I am the most magical creature on the face of the Earth who has access to limitless possibilities, I am still contributing to my legacy. However, I have a choice to decide if the legacy I will leave is one that makes me feel full of life and self-value or one that is bogged down by anger, resentment, and regret. Either way, having a child or not does not define one's legacy. Your legacy begins the day you are born.

What does this diagnosis make you feel about yourself - if you are infertile? Guilt. Anger. Sadness. Sorrow. Mostly, I feel like a victim to my body, to science, to genetics and to life. I feel like I got handed a raw deal and the lack of control about it all makes me feel powerless, not just in this struggle, but in life. It makes me feel like I am constantly on the defense and I have no real say in what is going to happen, so why even try to make things better?

What does this diagnosis make you feel about your partner - if they are infertile? In our situation, I feel a lot of the same emotions for him, which I feel about myself. Guilt. Anger. Sadness. Sorrow. I feel like I am robbing him of a life that he could have with anyone else. I feel like he is stuck in an undesirable situation and is trapped.

How do you feel about each other now – if you are infertile and they are not or vice versa? I love my husband. He is the best person I know. I worry that later he will look back on his life with regret because he stayed with a broken woman. I fear that he will resent me for stealing away the family that I know he so badly wanted. I carry shame that he has a wife who is infertile and have concern that one day he will not only stop loving me, but will find me undesirable. All of these fears aside, I am grateful that he is my partner and cherish the love and support he has shown me throughout our journey. I love him more today and each day it grows stronger and stronger despite the anxiety that exists in my head. I consider him to be the very best friend I could ever hope for and there is no one closer to me than him.

Are you both communicating your feelings about this situation to each other? Yes. I am now. I wasn't at first, and I can't explain why. I can make assumptions that it has to do with denial, fear, hurt, anger, and uncertainty surrounding how I felt about infertility, but I am very open, now.

Can you move on together considering a possibility that there may never be a baby - and, I mean EVER? Initially, my answer to this question was No. However, overtime it changed (and we will get more into that later), when I realized that I still have a life to live. Baby or no baby, I have this one life and if he isn't willing to move forward with me in living it, then I accept that. It'll hurt like a motherfucker, but I have to live for me and if that means he can't, then I love him enough to let him go.

Remember, there are no right or wrong answers when it comes to being introspective. If you're willing to take on the above questions, I suggest you find a quiet space where you can be present to what comes up without interruption. Write down your responses so you can go back and see what you wrote and where you're at with what you're going through, where you feel there is room to make progress, or to notice what might be a good place for you to start moving forward.

~

Whether you are struggling with symptoms or it is your partner, you need to determine how you or your partner being diagnosed "infertile" affects your lives as well as your emotional, mental, and physical selves. We will touch on this topic in further detail in stage three. For now, acknowledge that infertility affects you independently and as a couple but, before you move on to discussing options like surgery, IUI, IVF, or Holistic healing, recognize how this affects you first. I'm not suggesting you ignore your partners feelings but sometimes we get so hyped up worrying about someone else and their response to a situation that we don't take the time necessary to see how we're doing.

Ignoring your feelings can mean pretending it does not affect you and everything in your life. You are a lovely, nurturing, and thoughtful soul who cares about the wellbeing of your partner and your relationship but you aren't going anywhere quick if you don't know how you feel first. It is noble to assess their feelings and reactions, but there is no award or prize for doing so.

Asking someone else's opinion when trying to develop your own is useful when trying on clothes, making drastic hair changes, or eating something you think tastes funky. However, drawing a reactionary conclusion in life altering situations is a grave error. Not only does it cloud your judgment but it can also overshadow it.

While it is considerably important to understand how not having a child affects your partner, you will get there. Think about it. Every sperm needs an egg and vice versa so the conversation must be had. There's no escaping it unless... well, you're looking for a reason to escape, in which case, we'll touch more on that in stage three too, but I'd also urge that you may need a whole new book. Either way, in terms of your relationship, you need to decide what it means for you in your present before you can evaluate the effects it will have on you, your partner, and your future.

Here is where you decide if infertility means you are at a crossroads in your relationship and whether or not having a baby is a deal breaker and if you can move forward together regardless of the outcome?

Ultimately, while you're processing the "infertile" diagnosis, remember there is no baby yet. Or, if there is, and you're dealing with symptoms of secondary infertility, where you've already had a child but are struggling with a second conception, the point is to remember the life you have RIGHT NOW and not the coulda, shoulda, woulda. Before you put all your ovulation eggs in one basket and solely focus on "I want a baby!" remember to pause and see all the good you have because focusing on a baby more than each other can ruin an otherwise wonderful life and relationship. Take into consideration what exists in front of you and ask yourself if the life you live is enough to propel your relationship into the future.

What does this mean for your future? It means you need to stop worrying about it for feks sake! I know this is easier said than done with all the cycle watching, temperature taking, scheduled sexing, and cervical mucus touching but you must try! Focus on what your infertility diagnosis means in the present before becoming overwhelmed by how it affects your future because a lot happens in the future. A lot you don't know.

There's no guarantee you will have a baby as much as there is no guarantee you won't. I say this with peace and love but a baby is not the answer anyway. Remember, No Baby Band-Aids! The feelings you have as a result of your diagnosis will not be resolved with a baby. Yes, a baby may be your desired end result but I urge you not to rush past your feelings of sincere pain, of understanding, of considering what impact this diagnosis has on your life right this very second because, while they are undesirable, they are also important.

There is a lesson to the madness we encounter in life and for whatever reason this is your lesson. Believe me, I agree with every thought that says, "FUCK THIS." Truthfully, I do. I feel your anger and I see it comes from a broken heart. I see it is coming from feeling shock that this is not how your life was supposed to go. This was not a part of the plan and denying it is happening to you feels so much better than feeling enraged. Believe me, I get you!

Being angry or avoiding what is happening does not make it any less real. You will have to find the answers for yourself and it will be a mind fuck for sure. I'm not sugar coating it. Finding the lessons during times of suffering is unbearable. You will wage a mental battle trying to believe yourself when you say, "NO! I am not defined by my inability to have a baby. I'm a fulfilled human with a brain and a life. I am a confident and secure being who is a desirable sex goddess!" That is intended to make you feel as awkward reading it as I feel typing it to show you self-doubt is inevitable in this scenario and no amount of self-help proclamations will heal you. After all, self-help only works when you actually buy the bullshit you're ingesting.

You can't expect to stand in a mirror and tell yourself, "I will get pregnant" or "I am already pregnant" and expect it to be so when you're really thinking, "I can't get pregnant because we're infertile." Sorry. Self-help affirmations will not be your golden ticket to dealing and healing with infertility. You are the golden ticket.

Fact is you will be your own worst critic and enemy until you can develop acceptance over what is happening in your life. You will continue to deal with feelings of shock and denial that this is happening to you. You will continue to ask yourself questions to reaffirm who you believe yourself to be and, as you unknowingly evolve through healing, you will begin to see that what makes you happy does not reside in your future, it lives in the here and now. The only way to accomplish happiness through infertility is by accepting the shock that this is not what you had planned for your life, the denial that you refuse to accept it is happening, and let it teach you how you feel about it, all of it, in the present.

CHAPTER 8:
THIS IS HAPPENING
TO YOU.
IT IS NOT YOU.

By now, it's likely you're in a place of confusion. You receive the explanation of infertility as a reason you're not pregnant but you're not sure you understand what it means. You're not sure you accept it. You continue with a belief that you can overcome it and will not become victim to it but only in the sense that you get the outcome you want: a baby.

Having a baby is the ideal end result for anyone who struggles with symptoms related to infertility and discovers it as being the reason for unsuccessful pregnancy. This is true. What is also true; there are options available to you that may or may not help you to successfully conceive.

So, what happens if you don't? Considering the possibility that you overcome the odds and successfully become pregnant on your own is a positive outlook but engaging the idea that it may not work, that there are no guarantees in life, that science and medicine do not heal all wounds, does not make you negative. It makes you aware.

You can survive the emotional anguish brought on by infertility and you know that but you also know that you may never get pregnant and refusing all thoughts that suggest it does not make you damaged. Avoiding them is what does.

Month after month, menstruating becomes a constant reminder you're not pregnant and, with each period, you painfully realize infertility could be the reason. Up to now, you hoped to beat the odds but time confirms you do not. In failing to become pregnant, you begin to develop resentment for your present, this diagnosis, and all those who do not share your struggle. You yearn to understand why this is happening and each day hope turns into hurt. Eventually, all positivity sours and when hope, hurt, and confusion collide you become violently aware of the impact infertility has on everything you imagined for your life. This sudden consciousness is shock.

Initially, when shock floods your brain, you're generally haunted by the same series of questions.
Why is this happening to me?
How could this have been prevented?
What kind of life will I have if I can't have a baby?
What can we do to fix it?
I heard "Sally" struggled to get pregnant but she had success. Maybe, I'll get lucky too?

Life is not about luck and believing otherwise is what keeps you drowning in resentment, guilt, and self-blame. Luck is a disempowering concept. It takes all responsibility to your commitments and places it on the other side of the street with a mythical force that may or may not choose to shine its light upon you. It pulls you from a position of power in owning that some things work out and others don't, and allows us to avoid owning that truth. Believing that your circumstances are the result of good or bad luck leaves you feeling worthless when things don't go your way.

Let's take your friend, "Sally", for example. She struggled for 5 years to get pregnant and one day it happened for her. They stopped worrying, stopped using medication, and without even trying, she found herself pregnant. Now, after 5 years of struggling to conceive, suddenly she did. Isn't' she lucky? You, however, have been struggling to get pregnant for 2 years or even 10, with no such luck. You are unlucky.

I'm not saying that believing Sally's pregnancy luck is available to you is a *bad* thing. Sure. It can give you hope and faith that someday you will have the light of fortune shine upon you and grant you, too, this gift. However, what if it doesn't happen? What if lady luck never comes knocking for you? What then? Are you unlucky in life? Are you unworthy of a baby?

Luck is a tricky motherfucker because while it can give us hope and shift our focus from self-blame in the immediate present, when it doesn't shine it's grace upon us it can introduce a whole new set of self-blame into the mix that contributes to devaluing our self-worth. Quite frankly, no one needs help doing that.

Life is about circumstances, good, bad, blissful, or horrific. Sometimes, we make choices that impact us and other times we are reacting to how elements effect us. Either way, the recovery from both is not about luck. It is about choice and action. The choices we make that influence the action we take to deal or heal in life.

With infertility, in some cases, you're playing a long game. Overtime, questions can begin to build with the lack of answers or results. The longer it plays-out, it begins to affect more than just your decision-making abilities.

With each failed pregnancy test, uncertainty and randomness grow. Monthly menstruation or low sperm counts become too much to handle. This sort of overflow occurs when we are unwilling to experience pure emotion. Eventually, built-up frustration and resentment take hold of your emotional wellbeing and all that negative energy needs attention. You do have options here. You can make space for this negativity and use self-reflection to understand what drives it and find release or you can become a victim, acknowledge your aggressive feelings but refuse them, their presence, and do all you can to avoid feeling. The choice is yours.

Making space for our emotions allows them a place to grow. This can be a scary thought. However, in allowing their growth, we also find understanding and with that come awareness, resolution, and a way to make sense of it.

Refusing emotion is messy, messy, messy! I know. I did it for several years. It seemed like a good idea at that time and, quite frankly, I was very much convinced that I was pulling it off but my hair falling out, drastic weight loss, and explosive emotional eruptions would suggest otherwise. We'll touch more on possible emotional side affects of infertility later. For now, it is important to note that ignoring reactionary cues is like leaving a lit stick of dynamite in a gas station parking lot and walking away. It is flammable. It may take a while to see an explosion but there's likely to be fireworks!

No one wins when we're unwilling to tend to our internal negativity, namely us. In fact, doing so is when you transfer from fighter to a victim and without warning those bottled-up emotions can release as sudden outbursts. This can occur in the form of crying in the shower, crying in your car on the way to work, becoming enraged over laundry or emptying the dishwasher. Theses eruptions can make you look and feel insane. They are exhausting but more than that are a telltale sign something bigger is happening.

Sudden outbursts are your body's way of forcing you to realize your feelings are out of whack. That means screaming at your cat for shitting in the litter box is not exactly sane behavior. However, it is a signal that attention needs to be paid internally. It's a sign that, whether you like it or not, your emotions are coming to the surface and with them, prepare for spontaneous eruptions.

Having an emotional outburst may seem like something only crazy people do because crazy people can't control themselves but I've seen a few "sane" people lost their shit pretty good. Point is if you're feeling a little on edge and you can't control yourself, you may not be the C-word, I know I'm not supposed to say "crazy", but you're definitely going through something. I'd like to say, "Don't worry! This is a great sign." and give you the warm and fuzzies but, in the spirit of realization and healing, facing emotions can get ugly.

What are the ups and downs to processing your feelings?

The down side, because I always like the hard shit first, is processing emotions is never predictable or easy. It's messy. In an effort to protect your feelings, it is likely you could hurt others along the way. Don't worry! Unless you're a sociopath, none of this is intentional and as long as you don't stay the victim forever, you can come back from the dark side of the moon. Insert intentional Pink Floyd, shout-out!

The upside: Processing emotions will help you break down walls you've built that make you feel like no one could possibly understand what it is you're going through. Doing so will help you realize that blocking yourself from accessing your feelings and others from understanding you is not helpful. Again, you're not doing this because you're completely unable to relate to the emotions of others. It is because you're obstructing yourself from feeling anything because you are not prepared to deal with this shit and you're not ready to let them in.

Emotional outbursts, while less than glamorous, are a warning. Feelings are intense and unpredictable; therefore, some shit can go down. No one prepared me for this. Yes. I am aware that tough times often have difficult side-effects but no one told me that our struggle with infertility could have serious mental and emotional suffering. I wish someone would have been honest with me and drilled that into my head. I know it's not realistic to place all the blame externally but, admittedly, I had no idea the impact infertility would have on everything I am.

~

When I have my period, I'm pretty much a crazy person. I often compare it to a possession; physically, I'm still here, but mentally, Shannon isn't here right now, leave a message after the beep. However, having your period while also being doped-up on fertility hormones raging in your system is like a spiritual possession all together.

I was the Devil. There was no telling who would show-up to a conversation with me from minute to minute and 5 seconds later; it could be someone totally different. I felt like a nightmare, so being around me was probably no walk in the park.

On this particular day, I was what I would call 100% in my feelings. On top of facing another failed pregnancy, I was passing clot's the size of a silver dollar, my flow was bleeding through tampons within an hour, and the cramping that accompanied it made me feel like at any moment I was either going to die or deliver my uterus. I felt insane, emotionally unstable, and on this day I was both.

When I have my period I want carbs and cheese. In particular, pasta with swiss cheese. Not sure why? It's my thing. Some might say it is not the best thing for someone with Endometriosis and PCOS to have either of these, but when you feel like you're on your deathbed you make concessions.

Knowing how badly I felt, my husband came straight home from work and was taking the lead on making spaghetti for dinner. Yay, cheese and carbs! Also, yay husband! But, mostly, the cheese and carbs!

There I was sitting on the couch with a heating pad, my bottle of Tylenol and Advil, and a glass of red wine, when he set down my bowl of spaghetti. I picked it up, placed it on top of a pillow I had in my lap and began intentionally rolling my fork around in the sauce looking for cheese. When I found none, it felt like a fire had been lit inside me. I felt my body get hot and a giant sense of anger and disappointment filled me up. I didn't eat. Instead, I looked at him eating and stared.

Finally, after moments of glaring, he noticed and with confusion asked, "What's wrong babe?"

To which I responded, "Where the fuck is the fucking cheese, Scott?"

"Babe, I'm sorry. I forgot that I ate the last of the cheese and we didn't have any."

"Well, that's just fucking great, Scott! Per usual, you're only thinking about yourself. I wish I could just think about myself all of the time! Must be nice to be so self-centered."

"I'm sorry. It's just cheese, babe. I'll get more."
"It's not just fucking cheese, Scott!"

In the event you are equally unaware, and freaking out over dairy, consider this a courtesy warning. I love cheese too, but if you're doing this or things like this, friend, you need to reevaluate what is going on inside.

Don't worry. Freaking-out over trivialities is not exactly a sign that you've sunken into a deep abyss of psychosis from which you will never return. No. While you may love cheese, we're both aware that your fondness is not grounds for an argument. You're in a state of disarray where all your shit isn't exactly together. These are the breaks. Sometimes, we go through tough shit in life and there is no real way to prepare for it.

No one can prepare you for hard shit because we as people have a unique human response. As a result, I had no idea how fucked-up this struggle was going to make me feel but a little heads-up would have been nice. Again, this is your warning. However, this is also the part where I tell you honestly that I don't know if anyone gave me an alert and, even if they did, if I was capable of receiving it.

I've thought about this a lot, and as part of my healing, I agreed to stop casting blame on myself. I've agreed to stop shaming my body. I've agreed to stop defining myself by this situation. I've agreed to stop closing myself in and icing out my husband and family. I've agreed to stop looking for reasons of punishment in my life, past lives, and anything else. So, what does that mean?

It means, as difficult as it is to admit, maybe I wasn't open to receiving a warning or seeing the signs? Maybe, I had a one-track mind purely focused on a baby? Or, maybe, everyone wanted to be supportive and that meant telling me "I will get pregnant" even if there was a chance I would not.

I realize people want to be encouraging and there is an element of positive thinking that each doctor, practitioner, family member, or friend must maintain to keep the struggling person optimistic. Sometimes being hopeful is helpful for our sanity but hope does not diminish stress or the impact an experience can have on a person's health.

Not understanding how infertility could affect me, make me question my sanity, and feel alone in my struggle, only increased the strain it brought to my life and it is something I needed to hear, but didn't. Or, I maybe I did, but I couldn't accept it. I don't know and at this stage, I don't care.

What I do care about is truth. I think we all understand the motivation behind encouraging behavior. If you don't, then the simplest way I can define it is to inspire you to have faith in yourself more than you have doubt. It is to remain focused on the best outcome because we all want that in life. We want to feel like there is possibility things will go in our favor because it feels good and we know how to react to feeling good. To do this means we often refute or, at minimum, ignore that the negative exists because it feels bad and that means we are at risk for disappointment. I get why others feel a need to encourage us to have hope and it is the same reason we choose to do it. No one wants to be let down.

In particular, as it relates to things that can grossly adjust the trajectory of our life path, we are encouraged by others and enroll ourselves in believing we can have everything we want, exactly as we want it, all of the time. This is not good because it is not real!

Don't misunderstand me. I believe in the possibility to live a fulfilled life, but within must exist an acknowledgment that having happiness means also having disappointment too.

I'm not saying I don't believe in possibility. I'm not saying I don't choose to have more faith than I have doubt. Feeling good feels good and I want all the good feels too. I am suggesting we develop awareness around taking the good with the bad. I am saying that we need to be mindful about the unpredictability of life so when it places a giant crater between our ideal realities, instead of a crack in the pavement, it doesn't blow us out of our shoes.

There is power in taking action and making a commitment to have things go our way, while simultaneously, being alert to the fact that life will give us obstacles, and some of them might drastically shift that path. Taking this into consideration is not disempowering. It is powerful.

It allows us to know that we are capable of handling whatever it is that happens if things don't go according to plan. It helps us to feel the pain and acknowledge the disappointment, while also maintaining our sanity and all that prevents us from becoming destroyed when life throws a curve ball.

~

If I've learned anything in life, it is that honesty is always best. Honesty is hard. It can be painful and, sometimes, it is confusing but it is never wrong. No matter what has happened to me, I have never been unable to come to terms with truth.

Through cheating boyfriends, lying friends, malicious family members, and sheer stupidity, nothing in those scenarios ever turned-out good, because the lie always makes you feel that somehow you are undeserving of respect. While through the truth, no matter what happens, even if it is hard to take, it at least presents an element of regard for human decency.

There is a way to deliver bad news that makes it less shocking but, no matter what happens, it is going to be tough. Accepting that means having consideration for the person on the other end of it even if that person is you. Focusing only on the good is not sustainable, because as people we are flawed. We all die, cheat, hurt, and can be disappointed. Regardless of malice, life does what it wants so we might as well accept our responsibility to the truth even if it hurts.

When we ignore the truth, we open ourselves up to hurt. Let's look at it this way. If you lie, abstain from telling the truth, or if you are completely honest and tell the truth, either way there is potential for disappointment. While I believe that honesty is the best policy, I also believe that in order to be completely honest you must be transparent.

Take me, and this book, as a for instance. I accept that telling someone that they will feel "fucked-up" about infertility or anything for that matter could be counterproductive to their situation, especially since that may not occur, but it is honest.

Similarly, some may say it is self-indulgent to assume that your circumstance and the feelings that surround your reaction to it could mirror that of another's. I agree.

Where I disagree is ignoring that knowledge is power. I would say it is selfish to withhold information that might provide someone with insight or at the very minimum a sense of understanding. In other words, if you have experience or awareness around something, I think it is necessary to share it: good or bad. After all, what is absorbed from person to person is not fact. It is interpretation, so no use in not sharing.

For me, even if things never went sour and I had successfully conceived, it would have been helpful to know just how grueling the situation could have, and did, become. I think it is one of the reasons why so many people don't talk about their struggle with infertility. They think that something must be particularly wrong with them to feel this bad because you never hear anything about it. It should not be that way. I hope with this book that it is not that way any more.

I often tell people that I feel very strongly that there is a disconnect in the treatment process for infertility. There should be someone at each infertility treatment center who explains the mental anguish one can experience in his or her struggle. Maybe, there is a facility somewhere that I am not aware of which does this? But, there was no one like that where we sought-out care.

Again, I don't believe in the coulda... shoulda... woulda but I do believe having all the facts may have made me feel less alone and less like everything was my fault. Obviously, no one knew that I felt this way. I kept my feelings pretty silent but there is an element of honesty with infertility that is missing and having a little bit of it, no matter how resistant I was to hearing it, would have planted a seed.

Understanding how you feel is a process and sometimes it can feel long and confusing but knowing it and committing to engage it are two very different things. In our struggle with infertility, I wish anyone had given me a heads-up about the difference between feeling depressed due to our infertility diagnosis and understanding the factors that were contributing to it outside of not conceiving.

For instance, did you know that studies have shown a direct link between PCOS, anxiety and depression?

According to study results published in 2017 by the Massachusetts General Hospital Center for Women's Mental Health and information discovered in the Journal of Neuropsychiatric Disease and Treatment, research links anxiety and depression to women who were diagnosed with PCOS.

"The review explores the prevalence of psychiatric disorders between women with an established diagnosis of PCOS and those without PCOS. It concluded that depression and anxiety are more prevalent in patients with PCOS. Women with PCOS were nearly three times as likely to report anxiety symptoms compared to women without PCOS. Similarly, patients with PCOS were more likely to have depressive symptoms compared to women without PCOS."

Also, are you aware that Endometriosis also links to anxiety and depression?

According to a 2017 study published in the International Journal of Women's Health and referenced on EndometriosisNews.com, "Women with endometriosis have a higher risk of developing anxiety, depression, and other psychological symptoms."

The same web article goes on to note, "The association between endometriosis and psychological disorders has been reported in several previous studies, with depression and anxiety being the most common conditions. The incidence of such symptoms is higher in women with endometriosis than in any other gynecological condition."

This is just the tip of the iceberg. I can only imagine how the fertility medications play a role in enhancing the defeat felt with each failed pregnancy. Never mind adding the already linked anxiety and depression that come with symptoms related to infertility, such as PCOS and Endometriosis. Sadly, no one ever told me or talked to me about the impact either condition could have on my overall mental well-being or the role taking fertility drugs could play in enhancing depressive feelings. I really wish someone would have. It may have made me feel a lot less crazy.

Ultimately, with or without PCOS or Endometriosis, connecting to feelings about your struggle is a very delicate experience. You should prepare yourself to feel really raw in your emotions. They are likely to feel scattered, up and down, backward, and maybe even inside out. You will feel very all over the place along with them.

I'm sure this doesn't make you feel good but I tell you this so you don't feel alone. I tell you this so that if you do feel like you're spiraling out of control, you know that it is not just you. I tell you this so that you know the way to regain composure is to face the pain head-on, and to continue to unravel your pain, peeling back all levels of hurt one at a time, sometimes chunks at a time, until you arrive at healing.

~

Let me be the first to level set with you and tell you that it is a bitch. I tell you this not to scare you but because I wish someone would have told me.

Unveiling hurt is like watching a horror movie. You know something is hiding behind the curtain and you don't want to look but you're invested in watching, so even if you cover your eyes you leave a space between your fingers to see how the big-boobed girl is going to die. Then, just as you suspected, the hurt was hiding behind that curtain and boom... she's a goner.

Unfortunately, hurt... well, it hurts. There's no way to avoid it. It's like running up the steps in a horror movie; everyone who does this dies. Make a mental note now, "If a murderer ever runs into the house, do not run up the steps. Check!" Why? Because you can't avoid conflict!

Think about it, even Patrick Swayze said, "No one puts Baby in a corner." Do you know why? Because if there's a fire or some shit, Baby, is going to be the last to get around that table, and burn up like a tumble weed! Let's all take the advice of good'ol Patty Cakes and not put you in that corner either.

Whether you're fighting against a serial killer, preparing for a final dance sequence, or emotional self-destruction, you need to sit in a position of prominence in your life and be open to your feelings. You need to do this to deal with emotions whenever they strike because hiding from them or placing them in a corner can only lead to bad things.

Healing doesn't occur when we run away. It comes when we look difficulty in the face and say, "I'm scared as fuck but I'm more scared to continue living in a life that feels like dying." No. I'm not comparing infertility to death. Wait. Yes. I am comparing infertility to death. It is the death of a dream that said you were going to have a family and there would be no obstacle that stood in your way. However drastic this may seem, choose your death. Are you willing to feel like emotionally you're dying more each day? Or are you ready to try and face the impact, run head first into your fear, and mourn the death of how you thought 'happily ever after' would be?

~

As you transition from denial and shock, to shock and anger, you begin what I like to call "The Drunken Rollercoaster of Infertility". It's noisy, unpredictable, tosses you around, and makes you lose your center of gravity. It is very disruptive. This means you're going to feel all the bad, BAD, like really bad lows, go through the loops of emotional chaos, and keep fighting to live with that bad shit until you arrive at healing.

Don't confuse this with thinking the process goes from feeling bad to feeling good. Nope. Sorry. It's probably best if you just settle into the fact that infertility is a battle now. Doing so is unlikely to prepare you for just how hardcore it is but at least you're not expecting it to be a drive-by situation. I wouldn't compare it to being blown-up or anything that drastic but I would go as far as to suggest it's like having a rotting tooth in your head that needs specific and specialized attention to heal.

How do you prepare for infertility? Well, you don't. After all, there are not too many things we unwillingly go through in life that affect us inside-out, aside from disease, and, unfortunately, infertility is the kind of disease for which there is no cure.

If you're thinking there is a cure for infertility, no, there is NO CURE for infertility. You struggle from symptoms related to it or you do not. You can attempt to overcome it in whatever fashion you choose but treatment does not guarantee you will naturally get pregnant on your own. Even the surgical removal of symptoms relating to infertility does not guarantee you will become pregnant. If that were the case, I wouldn't be here with you but we will discuss options in stage five. That said, this will not be a bad to good scenario. Coming to terms with negativity is never easy or seamless and, given the depth of emotions involved with infertility, it will take time. The goal is to identify feelings, their source, and arrive in a place where you can have a genuine giggle and it feel really nice. Until that day, let us consider this process a drunken rollercoaster.

So far, what we know is the Drunken Rollercoaster of Infertility is unpredictable.

What we don't know is what that means? This means at any given moment, no matter what you're doing, you may encounter the following:

> You think about having a baby, your uterus, sperm, genetics, or your partner's penis, more than you care to admit... and this will happen multiple times per day for several days.

> While washing your hair, brushing your teeth, putting away laundry, or sitting on a conference call, you randomly tear-up or start crying because you may never carry and give birth to your own child... and this will happen multiple times per day for several days.

It's mid-afternoon, you're still in your PJs under a warm blankey with no lights, no TV, crying... alone... and this will happen multiple times per day for several days.

Perhaps, you're like me and you find yourself in a stage where you only want to watch horror movies or entertainment in which people could potentially die a horrible, painful, and bloody death... and this will happen multiple times per day for several days.

Whatever your coping mechanism, this dismality is actually a sign of progress. It means you are transitioning from denial and shock, to shock and anger. What's important is to recognize your hurt represents something: pain, frustration, confusion, or uncertainty. Whatever it reveals to you, ignoring it will only result in more hurt. Staying in those feelings does not help you heal and riding the wave to understand why they exist and where they come from is the only way to recover.

Stay with me here. Comparing the emotional struggle of infertility to being drunk and riding a roller coaster seems pretty accurate considering they're both a whole body experience. If you're afraid of heights, you can't take your eyes out to enjoy the ride any more than you can take your penis off to have a baby if you fear screwing-up the kid. For this example, let's consider the act of trying to have a baby the rollercoaster and the discovery of infertility as riding it drunk. Let me explain.

Trying to have a baby, much like riding a rollercoaster, involves committing to the activity for its duration. Unless, halfway through you decide that you no longer want a child. In which case, that is a different book and conversation. For now, we'll stick with those who want to have a baby and are committed to that. For all my dedicated baby makers, just like riding a rollercoaster, you know that once you're on the ride, there is no escape route. For those of you considering jumping the train or abortion, this is not a book about suicide or pro-choice vs pro-life. It is a book about struggling with infertility, so stay on topic. Both the act of trying to have a baby and riding a high-speed thrill ride look fun, yet slightly intimidating, considering there is no way to stop the train once it has begun. It's a commitment that leaves little room for changing your mind, but most, it not all, come out on the other side relatively happy.

Case in point, when people start the journey for baby, they're generally confident things will workout. They do the "deed," discuss if they can afford it, and whether or not they can keep it alive. While people who stand in line for rollercoaster's are not interested in deeding, they do conduct a different analysis of forthcoming events. Said "rider" reviews the severity of elements, discusses where to sit, how likely they are to enjoy it, and whether or not they can endure it without feeling like they will vomit or die. The intention of one is to produce human life while the other could leave you hoping yours won't end.

I find fertility and rollercoasters comparable because mentally once you're in it, there's no turning back. Well, not until the train reaches the station or you pop-out a baby. Either way, the intentions are to see it through to the end and that is usually true for most commitments.

When we mentally "green light" an idea, we are full speed ahead with it, giving minimal thought to difficulty or disruption. Often, it is this resolve that makes us successful but can also leave us ill prepared.

In the art of decision-making, there is generally something of fear or doubt involved and yet, in that, lives a thrill. Even if you have mapped-out the best to worst-case scenarios, there is no way to ever predict an outcome. Deciding to move forward, in any circumstance, dating, marriage, rollercoaster, new job, new house, car, moving across the country, or having a baby is a gamble. No matter what you choose, to stay or go, ride or not, try or not, each is a risk that could return unfavorable results. Good or bad, we chase the thrill because it is exciting!

There is excitement in achieving what we set out to accomplish. Whether it is reaching a goal, solution engineering a problem, overcoming a fear of heights, or having a baby, there is an element of adrenaline in the desired result. There is an element of pride, strength, and encouragement in our will to move forward in a direction and arrive at a meaningful end. For the most part, we are aware that the journey can be unfamiliar and potentially scary but we engage with hope that despite all unforeseen elements, things will turnout as planned.

As people, we are motivated by the pursuit of happiness and, whenever possible, use it to lead us to achieve an objective which is more of it and as much of it as possible. Pleasure is the thrill of life. If that weren't true, then people wouldn't have sex, jump out of airplanes, ride rollercoasters, or eat chocolate.

We don't *need* any of these to sustain living and yet we do them because we like to feel good. This feeling is addictive and we covet it because we like to feel satisfaction about our life and ourselves. It makes us feel as if we're doing something right, validates how we live, and gives us direction to continue to regenerate it in our lives and in the lives of others. Once this train of purpose leaves the station, there is no stopping it unless the car gets stuck or unforeseen circumstances strike. However, aside from unfortunate events in life, when we make decisions there is never any intention to pump the breaks until you're done or we get what we set out to achieve: happiness.

Happiness is the eternal drug. It fuels us in a way that makes us crave it like nothing else. Generally, we feel happy when things go our way and we don't have to do anything to engage those emotions. It comes naturally to us because it lives within us. Consequently, if it lives within us as a natural emotion, then so do disappointment, anger, sadness, depression, and fear. These emotions are in our arsenal and, simply by existing, they are who we are.

We typically encounter the opposition when things don't go as planned and, similarly, we don't have to do much to experience them either. Therefore, your likelihood to attain joy is equally as good as it is to any other emotion. As a result, we covet it and are in constant pursuit of it. Once it eludes us, or circumstances don't turnout, we're strung-out like a junky looking for a fix.

It's not wrong to want happiness or to have life go as planned. Nope. If it were, there would be a lot less toddlers losing their shit in Toy R'Us. However, just like a toddler who has been forewarned they will not get a toy, we do it. We commit to ideas or circumstances knowing full well things could get difficult or not workout. Even though we know it's not realistic to expect smooth sailing 100% of the time, we do it because it is far easier to commit to an idea of living happily then it is to imagine anything else.

It is right to be hopeful and believe that you will be happy. You should live that way. You deserve it. In fact, we all do and there is no reason not to. However, it is also either ignorance or in thinking you have accounted for all possible outcomes that allow us to make decisions and dive headfirst, expecting nothing less than success. We do this for the same reason we believe we are entitled to happiness because it is sad not to and no one wants to be around unhappy people.

Before you roll your eyes and get all high and mighty on me, think of the last time you craved time with someone who was going to talk about everything wrong in life. Oh, never? Okay, then, Mother Theresa, let's keep going.

Believing life is predictable and welcoming the thrill of it but also living with an attitude of "that won't happen to me" is not what keeps you happy. Yes. Choosing to believe that we will not be affected by life's unforeseen dismality, which is available to all of us, does not leave us feeling hopeful and sexy about our future. In fact, conflict avoidance actually serves a purpose for the optimistic. It is what keeps you ignorant and allows you to expect life to unfold as anticipated.

Don't think of your ignorance as a constant negative. It can be a good thing too as long as you're not caught shoplifting because you were unaware that the "five finger discount" did not apply to you. It can be the thing that propels you to take messy action in your life, to achieve a goal, defy the odds, and succeed when the universe gave you every reason to give up. However, it can also be the reason why we follow our heart and wind-up heartbroken because we took a risk while disregarding the consequence.

There are consequences for us all and claiming ignorance is the reason you broke the law after the age of 6 is not something I think will hold up as a criminal defense. It does, however, allow us to live in the moment and leap, as well as believe the bullshit metaphor that says you can build a parachute on the way down and survive.

First, no one carries that amount of fabric and, second, the ability to sew mid-air is some Wile E. Coyote and Road Runner shit. Since we're not cartoons or birds, I think we can all agree that thinking you can succeed at every chance you take is reckless. Also, and I say this with peace and love, it is fucking stupid, unless, of course, you are a bird. Not sure if you're a bird? Do you have feathers? No? Then, you're not a bird and you shouldn't jump out of an airplane or off a building without a parachute. Capeesh? Ultimately, being happy is a thrill in and of itself and it allows us to compare the exhilarating rush of leaping from treacherous heights to that of taking a risk on ourselves for happiness. We will do anything to attain it including believe we can defy whatever odds are laid out before us.

Let's be real. We are painfully aware that there is a lot of shit in the world to be unhappy about. When we set forth on a path to achieve a goal, whether it is surviving the worlds tallest coaster or successfully creating a human, we do it because we live for this shit and contrary ideas have no place in an optimistic world of possibility.

What does have a place in this optimistic universe? If you guessed ignorance as the only quality available in an optimistic existence, then that is 500 life points for you! It allows us to focus on having everything go our way. It permits us to believe that nothing could possibly go wrong while riding a rollercoaster upside down, 1000 feet in the sky, at 70mph, wearing a fabric seatbelt, and holding your hands in the air like you just don't care.

Truth is, whoever coined the saying, "Ignorance is bliss," hit the nail right on the head. There is no predicting who will meet tragedy versus those who seemingly live happily ever after, because life is all about chance. It's not about who is the most ignorant lives the happiest. Or whoever has children leaves the most fulfilling legacy. Or who was given the most information is the most prepared. Nope. We roll the dice hoping for the best even if we know something could go wrong because happiness and ignorance are both a choice we choose.

Happiness is not a quality that exclusively grows from truth. If that were the case, there would be no student loans, credit cards, mortgages, or car loans. We're constantly taking chances on ourselves believing our ass will be able to write a check that can be cashed each month in order to afford how we live. We choose to be ignorant of the fact that we could lose our jobs tomorrow and wind-up in an insurmountable amount of debt. We take the risks because we want to believe we are capable of receiving the reward.

It is the same goes for everyone who buys a home. We do it because it elevates us to feel a sense of accomplishment not because we're thinking about bankruptcy. In fact, we aren't thinking about the negative at all and yet, there is a part of us that should. If someone were to tell you that you're likely to draw a short straw the next time you dare to do something, the truth is you wouldn't be holding your hands in the air like you just don't care. You would ditch daring and hold onto that safety belt with a death grip because you would care. You would care a lot!

The same goes for making the decision to have a child. We do it because it is thrilling, fulfilling, and full of promise! For some, it elevates our egocentric existence and provides purpose. We take the plunge and choose to believe that nothing could go wrong, because thinking otherwise is labeled as living in fear, and, in today's society, that is bad. I don't know why. I don't really see awareness of all possible outcomes as fearful but mindful. For instance;

> What if while riding a rollercoaster you vomit but what if you don't? Would you choose not to ride because you could throw up? You could also throw-up from eating too much chocolate. Would you stop eating chocolate forever because of the possibility?

> What if while trying to have a baby you discover you suffer from symptoms related to infertility? Would it change your decision to try because it might not work? You could defy the odds and get pregnant. Would you stop wanting a child and forego sex because you discover it could be hard?

When we mentally commit to something, our body, hearts, and everything we are follows. This happens because we want to be happy and, in the pursuit of happiness, we lay all that brings us joy on the line side-by-side with ignorance for the thrill of achieving what we have committed to. Whether it is the adrenaline rush that comes from thrusting yourself towards the ground at an ungodly speed or becoming a parent, we commit to it for no other reason than we decide we want to. We are determined beings. Sometimes that determination is enough to propel us toward real greatness because it is driven by happiness. Whether our drive is fueled by emotion or experience, having a thrill or a baby can be both.

~

It takes a lot of nerve to pursue anything in life and the bravery it takes to stick it out, stay the course, and keep going despite naysayers, conflict, or struggle is the rollercoaster. Being drunk is when persistence, thrill, and determination do not waver when maybe they should. Being drunk is choosing to continue the ride without taking a moment of pause to evaluate how the situation has changed, how it has already impacted you, and in what ways it could affect you if you continue. Being drunk is when we forge ahead in pursuit of a goal considering all elements of a situation have not changed although we know it has. Being drunk is choosing to believe that not only the circumstances are unchanged but so are we.

I'm not saying persistence and choosing not to give up on something you believe in or believe will give you happiness isn't a levelheaded decision. I certainly believe that we should do whatever possible in the pursuit of happiness. This is your life and you only get one shot at it. However, I do not believe a clear mind chooses to move forward with a plan exactly as it was before all cards were dealt and pretend it is the same game.

I believe a level head knows when to pause and reevaluate the situation, consider what is at stake, and doesn't refuse to quit simply because playing to win is more pleasant than feeling a loss. No. No one likes to lose and we like it less and less the more it impacts our life. However, the truth of the matter is that sometimes in life we lose and it sucks really fucking bad but there is a difference in pursuing something because it is essential to your existence and pursuing it because you are afraid to engage thoughts of who you are if you don't have it.

In pursuit of a goal, we are seduced by it the minute we engage it and accept it into our life. Generally, we are not only driven by it but the allure of it. We manifest in our mind how much better life will be once we accomplish it. Not only is it important to us but also it changes how we see ourselves and how we believe others will see us too. In some capacity, it becomes who we are and we become it. With this, there is very little room for opposition or negativity.

To entertain contrary thoughts is unconscionable because it would challenge our progress, our ideal reality, and how we identify ourselves in a life where everything works out in the end. Therefore, we develop a mentality that will not and cannot accept defeat. We will sacrifice money, relationships, and ourselves to level up and realize this elevated existence. We risk it all for mental, emotional, and personal success because we believe that is what it takes to get to our best life. I agree with this. I agree that we need to take big risk to receive big reward. However, I also believe that sometimes we don't know when to give up and sometimes taking too much of a risk for future gain comes at a detriment to our present.

I don't know that I would say our inability to see when we've gone too far is because we're too stubborn, idealistic, or spoiled. I think it might be simpler. It might be because it is a challenge to change who we are even if who we are hasn't materialized yet. In other words, just because we haven't reached a goal doesn't make the payoff any less real to us.

Committing to something is more than mental. Whether its surviving a rollercoaster or successfully creating or conceiving a human, when we set out to achieve something, disappointment is generally an afterthought because the desired end result has only one possible outcome and that is victory.

When we make a decision it is real and personal. Typically, that choice comes with varying levels of thought and all revolve around the potential for success. In our pursuit, achieving the objective is only half of the desired outcome. The other half exists in believing that we have already achieved it and so we are all, Alicia Silverstone, living "as if", and operating under the mindset that we have succeeded.

We have absorbed how we imagine it will feel to live in a reality where we are the person who sets out to do something and does it. These are all crucial behaviors of successful people. No one who has ever achieved anything in life has set out with a mentality that they wouldn't but many of those same people have failed and faced life-altering disappointments as well.

To say it is a disappointment when our goals do not materialize is an understatement. Avoiding defeat could very well be the reason we push ourselves too hard, don't know when to quit, and sacrifice more than we should to succeed. We reject the idea of failure because that means we would need to figure out who we are if we don't succeed and that is slightly difficult to do when we're already basking in the euphoria of success.

The challenge here exists in saddling the line between being painfully optimistic and crucially realistic. We can fight for something to happen all day long, and for years on end, while still having awareness that at some point we may need to abandon ship. I know we don't like to hear the negative but sometimes facing it is what allows us to become our best possible selves. Discovering how to cope when things don't go as planned and finding acceptance in that is a difficult thing to do when we are chained to a reality where everything works out. This is where we can get into trouble.

~

Our greatest tool is optimism; it can help us to persevere and stay afloat in the worst of times but it can also be the anchor that keeps you chained to a sinking ship and pulls you under. The balance comes in knowing when to keep treading water and fighting to stay afloat versus knowing when to cut your ties and fight for your life. Understanding this could mean happiness will need redefining. The goal will need revisiting and a determination must be made on whether or not it is attainable. This is where things can become sticky.

If you find that things aren't going as planned, this may be an opportunity to pause and reevaluate what the future can look like for you now. The unavoidable truth is that if the situation has changed then you are no longer capable of pushing forward without knowledge of the presence of an obstacle. No matter how much you want to pretend a challenge hasn't presented itself, you cannot proceed as if things are unchanged. If you decide that you are uninterested in engaging the facts and the thought is that you can't be happy until you succeed, this is where you can become drunk: drunk on happiness, the chase for it, and achieving it.

Being drunk is the "liquid courage" guzzled down and brought forth by our ego It is what convinces us to keep going. It is what encourages us to see past the resistance despite knowing something is not right. It is what allows us to disregard feelings of guilt, fear, anger, depression, and in its place create a need to move forward, do more, try again, and stay consistent. It convinces us that if we stop now, or don't continue, then we'll regret it, be to blame, or have ruined our own happiness, because we were too lazy, weak, or selfish to continue. It drives us to forge ahead, but intoxicates our mind with a fear-based certainty. A certainty that says, if we stop now we are a quitter and we will miss out.

The ego is not a terrible thing. In the hands of believing anything is possible, it gives us hope, power, exhilaration, and confidence. However, in the hands of fear, it can be the difference between taking mindful action from your heart and haphazard action, because anything seems better than nothing.

It convinces us that our best, happiest, most fun, or fulfilled life is in that extra cocktail, 1 more hour of work, all inclusive vacation, investment in the stock market, or belief that a doctor or science has the cure to fix you, your pain, your loved ones ailment, or even infertility. It's empowering, radical, and encouraging, because at any time it can go from being the best risk on happiness you ever took, to the risk that takes happiness from you.

The fact of the matter is there is no key to happiness, but there is choice.
Is what I am doing making me happy? Yes or No. Choose.
Does my relationship make me feel fulfilled? Yes or No. Choose.
Are the actions I take seeing the progress I want? Yes or No. Choose.
Can I go on living my life this way? Yes or No. Choose.
Am I the sum of my struggles with infertility or am I much more than that? Yes or No. Choose.

Life is a shot in the dark, and most of us are doing the best we can to choose wisely. Sometimes we choose to act from love, and other times we run head first into a wall over and over again, because we're too afraid to give up, take pause, or level set with what the fuck it is we're trying to achieve and how we're choosing to do it.

The truth is we've all done this in some capacity or another. We feel trapped. We feel isolated. We feel misunderstood, and so we move forward doing the best we can because we think it is the "right thing" to do.

I'm not saying we do this all the time. I'm not invalidating your choices. I'm not saying coming from love is better than choosing from fear. Hell no! Do what works for you!

What I am saying is if you feel like you're doing things for the sake of doing them, and you don't feel like your heart is the driving factor, or you don't know what in the actual fuck you are doing, then there is no shame in your game if you take a pause!

We push forward believing that satisfaction exists within doing something else or being something more sometimes, because we simply don't know what else to do. We believe that to give up means we are failing ourselves or forfeiting a life of joy, and, in doing so, our unhappiness is our own doing. Therefore, we convince ourselves that the only way to find fulfillment it is to keep going even if something feels off.

Why do we do this? Ehh, I guess you could say it is the pursuit of happiness or the fear of failure or maybe ego. In my opinion, who the fuck cares about the *why* if you know it's making you unhappy. I'm more concerned with the *what*. As in, what do you choose next? Because, no amount of belaboring over the choices of the past will change them once you have awareness to them, they will always be what they were and are. The opportunity lies within noticing what is and deciding what you are committed to do next.

No matter the amount of conflict, resistance, or grave devastation we potentially face when making a commitment, most of us will strap in, remain seated with hands, arms, legs and feet inside the ride at all times. Some might say it is this self-promise that keeps us committed to our commitments despite all signs of impossibility. Some might say it is the fear of giving up or quitting too soon and missing out on the piece de resistance. Others might say that it is far greater to have hope and believe in the unknown, than it is to live a pessimistic life. I would say it's perhaps a bit of it all.

I have found that if the going gets tough and we do not get going it's because we're too scared to look at how we can take accountability to create happiness in the face of uncertainty. We either become paralyzed with knowledge of how damaging bad news can be to our happily ever after, or we do everything we can to distance ourselves from the pain and power through it. For example, we may do one of two things.

One, we stay in our comfort zone out of fear. In this instance, the fear of unknown holds us back, so we stay in it, doing what we know will make us happy, while still lusting after something that requires us to think, speak, or act different. Here we fall out of integrity with our happiness by neglecting to be honest with ourselves about how anxiety of the circumstance is paralyzing our ability to see that there are choices to be made which can help us move forward. Instead, we stay where we are and refuse to see how we're contributing to our own unhappiness in addition to any damaging external elements.

Two, we take a giant leap outside of our comfort zone while acting like a kamikaze. From this place, the fear of the known pushes us to act reckless and disregard what is presently causing our unhappiness. We obsess over it, while also trying to ignore it. Here, chasing happiness becomes the goal, instead of being present to what is causing our discontent. We convince ourselves that we are miserable because of circumstances out of our control. We wildly pursue anything to counteract those emotions, while still lusting after something that requires us to take accountability for how we are reacting to it. Here, we fall out of integrity with what we want, because we thrust ourselves into the unknown with ignorance, not awareness, and use action as a means to cover up or side step what is creating pain.

In life, your goals are the rollercoaster, and pursuing goals in the face of well-known obstacles is riding it drunk. You grow by experiencing the highs and lows in life, and so do your goals. As you change, they change. For all the foreseen highs, there are gut wrenching and unpredictable lows. You don't need me to tell you that life is unpredictable. We all know that. What is important to consider, and we often don't, is our limits.

We see limitation as weakness and perceived failure as fear. We all look at ourselves as if we're invincible because for some reason the alternative is almost inconceivable. After all, what makes us think we're deserving of going-out into the world and making a million if we so choose to do it? I'll tell you: invincibility. We believe in our ability to achieve whatever we set our mind to and we should. However, what we don't consider is the possibility that we won't be able to achieve it and sometimes we are ill prepared to deal with an emotional overhaul we cannot escape when things don't go as planned. So, instead of abandoning the ship, we hold on and, come hell or high water, we are bound and determined to make it sail despite the fact that instead of floating we are actually sinking.

Life is crazy enough. The last thing you need to do is walk around drunk, out of control, and unaware of what is going on around you. Considering you have committed to the dream of having a family some day, and the decision is that it will be soon, makes the experience of achieving it important. Thus, you strap on your safety belt and prepare to enjoy the ride. You anticipate unexpected elements and often refer to them as surprises but what is not expected is being stopped dead in your tracks with news that the ride will not go as planned and may not happen at all.

Fertility is a rollercoaster. There are many ups and downs, unpredictable twist and turn, and, as I said, the ride does not stop until you commit to it. There are so many hard truths about infertility and a major one is, if you want kids, but unfortunately, you're infertile, that may not happen. That right there is a mind-fuck in and of itself. Add to it that you are the reason you can't have something you want and you become numb to all of it. Why? Well, who the hell wants to feel like they're the reason for their own discomfort? It's like being told you will be locked in a room with all the things in life you hate except it's just you. You're it, the thing you hate and you can't get away from yourself, because well, you're you. You're the problem. You're a walking, talking, living, breathing, eating, sleeping problem. And, if that's not enough to throw at you... there's not a damn thing you can do to change it. FUCK!

And again, sometimes you need to say fuck.

Why does infertility make you drunk? Sometimes when we're drunk we do random and out of character things. The same goes for shock and denial. When drunk, sometimes you're in denial of how drunk you are until you vomit or the next morning when you wake-up to a pounding headache

Being in shock and denial is basically conflict avoidance. It means we know something is there (i.e. you're drunk, stop drinking) or could potentially exist (i.e. you're an emotional wreck, stop ignoring it), and we actively choose to deny its presence. That's where we live in stage one of our infertility diagnosis, taking shot after shot of shock "how did this happen to me", and swallowing chunks of denial "this is NOT happening to me" while trying not to vomit.

When we begin to acknowledge what infertility means to our life plan and relationships, like a rollercoaster on its way to a hangover, drunken denial and shock quickly progress to shock and anger. This is where you try to push your feelings down so deep you think they aren't noticeable or affecting you but you're actually an emotional wreck.

Being an emotional wreck, we often make haphazard decisions that in the moment seem super awesome but aren't necessarily the best for us in the long run. You know, like riding a rollercoaster drunk!

Find comfort in knowing there is no way you could have prepared for this. We'll talk more about this in stage four but, for now, know you responded the best way you knew how. You had an ideal fairytale in your mind about how life was supposed to turnout for you so it's not completely ridiculous that you just reacted when you found out it wasn't going to play out that way.

When unfamiliar life-altering situations present themselves, there are very few people who know immediately how to get in and out of it unscathed. There is nothing you could have done to prevent this scenario. Don't beat yourself up over it, just sit, take it like a champ, and commit to being unhinged for a while because once you accept how infertility is affecting your life it escalates rather quickly.

When does this ride end? The train is tracking uphill and as you absorb its momentum with each click-click-click you get flashes of your life and all the things you wanted prior to infertility:
9-months of fear "the good kind",
the parent you would have been,
what your baby would look like,
what delivery is like,
if the doctors are wrong,
if the doctors are right,
and what if you can't go on in your life?

Just as you begin to think if you can live a life like this, a flash WARNING sign with red letters appears at the top of hill. You think, "WARNING? Now a WARNING?!"

The WARNING reads, "This ride will never end. You will deal with it everyday for the rest of your life. It is a part of you."

This gives you a moment of pause. "Hello, Shock. Is that you again?" Your heart sinks and as you start to feel Anger creep-in, the car crests, and your stomach drops as you fly down the hill.

CAUTION: Shock and anger will teach you how to identify what is jarring about your diagnosis and why it is coupled with rage. Shock and anger are exhausting, confusing, and take a lot of energy. They're good and bad.

Shock and anger are bad because they keep you "in your feelings." Living in shock and anger cause tunnel vision and a state of still. It's difficult to make mindful and heartfelt choices when the mind and heart are buried under strong feelings. It's difficult, but not impossible. Together, they create a block from a positive present and lock you in the hurt of your diagnosis. It is not healthy for you to stay here but it is helpful for you to feel it if you do.

Shock and anger are good because they offer hopeful resolution to feelings of despair. Living in shock and anger help you see the source of your pain. Yes. Some crazy shit happens along the way. Yes. You can develop fits of unfamiliar wrath. Together, they can create an unavoidable mirror of truth.

When you realize there is a difference between understanding your feelings and hiding in them, you will find resolve. In allowing yourself to feel slight, hopelessness, outrage, and numbing pain, you may begin to feel like you're in a downward spiral into depression but you will also uncover release. Until you can align with your desperation, ignoring feelings of shock and anger will keep your ass glued to that rollercoaster seat and riding the emotional wave. To help you process your feelings of defeat, we'll get into some helpful affirmations in bit, but for now let's take on some anger!

147

~

Ever been stung by a bee? Well, for the purposes of this book, we will assume you have. Cool – me too! That's shock and anger in a nutshell. It stops by, scares the shit of out of you, hurts a bit, makes you angry and leaves you alone to deal with the aftermath. The only difference between a bee sting and infertility is that we know the bee will die after it stings you, and if you're anything like me, that gives you a bit of satisfaction. Whereas with infertility, there's no knowledge of what will or won't happen following your diagnosis, and that leaves you with a lot of anxiety and very little contentment.

Infertility is a relentless disease. It swoops in, hits you with a bomb of fear, confusion, disbelief, and leaves you holding a big old bag of what the fuck just happened. I call this denial. We ride the wave of denial and this isn't happening to me, as a way to pacify our overwhelming emotions. That is, until we can no longer numb ourselves to the circumstance, and our temporary response is taken over by feeling.

Denial is what allows you to go on thinking this is a mistake, the doctors were wrong, and everything will be ok. It is also the thing that might enable your persistence. Consider it a buffer to reality.

I'd like to tell you that living in denial is impermanent, but I've met a lot of people who I think live in it, so I won't overgeneralize here. What I will say is if you're trying to successfully conceive and have been advised that you're struggling with symptoms related to infertility, and choose not to believe it, then you may be in denial.

On the other hand, if after an extended period of time you don't find yourself pregnant, but are increasingly frustrated, bitter or angry, well, that is when I will assert your denial has ended, and where shock and anger will pick-up speed.

Simply put, shock and anger are awareness. They don't have to mean anything bad. In fact, I would encourage you to view them as a consciousness. Shock is a reaction and anger is a feeling. Badda-bing! Badda boom! It's that easy!

Shock allows you to ingest that what you have been told, and are currently avoiding, is possible. It doesn't mean you have accepted it, or that you will never have children, or even that you won't try to have them. No. It is a sudden response to what infertility can mean for you and how it might impact your future. It is an awareness that stops thoughts from saying *this isn't happening to me,* and changes it to *why* is this happening to me?

If shock is the gateway to feeling, then when the reality or pain of what you feel emerges, anger can be the realization that comes through. Again, anger doesn't have to be *bad*. It can be unpleasant, that is for sure, but it is a feeling. It is an intense emotion that represents your response to a current circumstance.

It's not wrong and it's not right, but it can be what comes up when you realize that what you thought would never happen to you, was wrong, or *isn't happening,* is, and whether the emotion is directed at you, your doctor, parents, spouse, partner, uterus, ovaries, sperm or friends, it is a sign of vulnerability and a reaction to a situation.

Vulnerability is a complex emotion. We often associate being vulnerable with being weak, sad, or as a term used only in relationships. I see it as an expression of feeling. When you are vulnerable, are you are not aware that you are? Yes. Similarly, when you are angry, are you not also aware? Again, badda bing, badda boom! It's that easy.

Denial, shock, and anger, are simply responses. They are not right or wrong, but they can be useful indicators that you are progressing through something. They are not numerical and follow no particular order, so you may experience one but not all or all but in varying ways, and there is no finish line, so please don't see them as a telltale sign of healing. They are unpredictable and particular to the human experience.

Similar to a rollercoaster, feelings, thoughts, and emotions are not linear things, and often there is forward, backward, upside-down and right-side-up progress, so encountering denial once does not mean you will never encounter it again. And, encountering anger does not mean you can't then encounter denial or shock or something different later on.

The point is, responding to grief is like riding a rollercoaster. Even if you have all the information and can see the track laid our before you, or know that it is a high-speed ride and understand that the journey ahead can be difficult, you cannot predict the outcome and you do not know with complete certainty how you will respond to the varying levels of it's intensity. It is an all or nothing commitment, with very little control and a whole lot of risk.

~

When you begin to realize feelings of anger and identify with them, it doesn't just beg to be identified. It demands to be processed. In other words, it is not enough just to find the problem but you need to love it back to health.

In the history of arguments or conflict, nothing was resolved without a little TLC. If you don't love yourself past your pain, you will continue to LIVE IN IT. You must find a way to forgive yourself and your situation or you will drown in it. Don't know how? I'm going to help you. In the words of Dori, "Just keep swimming."

I wish I could tell you this was all a dream and at any moment you will wake-up.
I wish I could tell you that tomorrow or the next day it won't hurt anymore.
I wish I could tell you that the doctors are wrong.
I wish I could tell you why you have been chosen to endure this.
I wish I could make all feelings of inadequacy go away.
...but I can't.
It sucks writing it and it sucks feeling it.

You know in your heart of hearts neither of us have answers to any of the above or the millions of questions that will follow throughout your struggle. I want to be able to tell you that this will be better soon but that is entirely up to you. I hate that it seems like such a simplified response but it's true and somewhere inside of you, you know it.

I want nothing more than for you to find your joy again. I want you to wake-up and have a morning where your first thought isn't about how sad, alone, and unworthy you are but I can't grant that. What I can do is tell you that if you want those things you're going to need to find them.

Until you decide you're ready to turn down the volume on all the thoughts that make you feel inadequate and purposeless, and turn up the volume on those that say, "I am more than this" and "I will live a happy life", I will simply say this is your party and you can cry if you want to. In fact, it's inevitable. You will cry.

If you're in this place where you feel life sucks and you hate yourself, everyone else, and still think about screaming, "Fuck you, Baby!" at short people, then you are in this until you decide how to cope, deal, or don't let it run the show anymore. That's precisely why you need to go through it because going through it will allow you a chance to heal.

~

Tough love: this is your life. You have been diagnosed with infertility. Yes. But you are NOT infertility. This isn't runny eyeliner or a pair of boxer shorts that gives you a wedgie. It's not something you went out to purchase, discovered it was faulty, and can return in 60 days for an exchange or a money back guarantee. This is a part of you or your partner. The point is the sooner you start realizing that this is not something you contracted, the sooner you may start realizing there is nothing you could have done or can do to change your diagnosis.

Affirmations to help you stop your Adult Child-sized Tantrums, help you align feelings of hopelessness, introduce truth with levity, and forgive yourself for being infertile.

I did not ask for this.
I did not contract this or bring this on myself.
This is not happening to me as some form of punishment.
This does not mean I am a worthless partner or will get a divorce.
There is nothing in my life I could have done to make this different.

The basic summarization of this scenario is a sperm and an egg came together to create you. You became a baby and you were born. YEA! In the words of Thomas Dolby, "I just blinded you with science" … you're welcome! In short, your lady or gents parts were created exactly the way they were created. No one can go back and inject "better" sperm or give you more eggs. No one can go back and remove your endo or PCOS or scar tissue or reverse premenopausal conditions, testicular, cervical, or ovarian cancer.

I am not diminishing you down to genetics or circumstance and You Shouldn't Either.

You're freaking amazing! I don't know you personally but I can guarantee, if you sat down and thought about it, you have at least 5 people in your life that believe you are the "bees knees." Or, a boss that thinks you work your ass off and don't know what they'd do without you. Or, a sibling that looks up to you and knows you make their life better. So, friend, end this nonsense right now and let's put a motherfucking cabash on the minimization of all that makes you a miraculous, bunch of magical, delight, because you are!

Whatever circumstance exists in your situation, I am sorry. I am so fucking sorry, it makes my heart want to leap from my chest and envelope you in all the love I already have for you. That said, I have to give you the harsh truth with peace and love; we can't change what happened, so don't you waste one more minute of your beautiful existence believing you are the sum of your circumstance, because it is a lie!

Who you are is undeniably the most beautiful part of your life and if you are not in a position to realize it right now, then you are missing a magical life. Your *youness* is unique and very necessary to the world. Having people in your life that value you is great, but when you value you life is infinitely better!

You are all the things that give the universe value. You have qualities of goodness that you bring to life just by being. They're important to others and they all occur because you're you. Don't you dare begin to minimize the validity of your existence down to infertility.

There are options to pursue to have a baby but a baby is not a Band-Aid and having one does not reverse the truth of your circumstance. Understanding our anger helps us to own our value and you add value whether you currently believe it not, because infertility sucks, but you do not.

Infertility is a disease that is afflicting you. You are not a disease. You are a person living with it and adjusting to that life as best as you can. What you need to do is ingrain in your mind that you are not infertility. If you need to say it to yourself multiple times per day until you start ingesting it, then do it. What you don't need to do is drink the victim Kool-Aid and start looking for answers where they do not exist or spout off accusations.

Don't yell at your mom for Endo.

Don't blame your dad for holding you upside down too much as a kid.

Don't accuse your parents of serving you too many microwaved foods.

Don't overanalyze the number of hot tubs you've frequented in life.

Don't and I say this with the utmost sincerity, do not wish you were never born.

These and other thoughts are crazy. Yes, I know I'm not supposed to use the C-word but dammit they are and I love you too much not to tell you.

If you're giving infertility the power to diminish your value by drinking the victim Kool-Aid, trust me when I tell you that no one is going to have an answer for you as to why you are the "chosen one." This is your story. This is your body. No amount of blame or crafty storytelling is going to make it any different.

~

I get that drinking the victim Kool-Aid is hard to avoid. We want to be angry when we're angry. We want to be justified in our anger. We want to punch something and mean mug some babies, but we can't do those things. Why? Because, they're the C-word, and in your heart of hearts you know that.

You can have days where you want to be angry but allowing yourself to stay in that place too long is like a black hole to a galaxy far, far, away. You run the risk of going in and never coming out. So my recommendations on being angry are:

Don't "Jim Jones" yourself! For those that don't know, I'm going to save you a Google trip. Jim Jones was an American cult leader who forced a bunch of people to oppress themselves by thinking they were victims. The outcome was very tragic as in all but a handful of people died. Moral, if you drink the *why is this happening to me* victim-Kool-Aid, know that we all do sometimes, but you must snap out of it sooner rather than later. Avoiding what oppresses you will not heal you.

Don't walk into the black hole of anger and stay too long. Remember what happened to the girl in "The Ring" who fell down that dark well? Yeah. She looked rough afterwards. Trust me. From someone who lived this, if you rent a room at the Black Hole Inn, one day you'll walk in and before you know it, it's 4 years later and you've missed a huge chunk of your life. Sometimes, when we resign ourselves to something, even if it's bad for us, it becomes comfortable. Do Not Become Comfortable In Your Anger. It will consume you and take over your.

Don't close out the world. Talk about your feelings. I get that communicating them to your partner or family is difficult, but is it any harder than feeling like you live in 24/7/365 isolation? In sharing your feelings, it can mean you're processing them, which is fantastic! It also means you're in a place where you understand how you feel about what you're going through, which is otherworldly amazing. #3 will take time because we all process things at our own pace but, if you're looking to get out of a depressed rut, this is something to shoot for. After all, sharing is for caring and trust me what I tell you that if you are hurt, then your loved ones are hurting for you, too. It may feel like this is only affecting you but trust me when I say: it is not all about you, my friend. Love is a circle and the people who love you feel your pain. No one likes a one-sided relationship and nothing is more one-sided than icing out those you love. Nurture yourself and your circle of trust, by letting those who love you in!

Point is take some time to be angry while digesting your anger so you can heal. Your feelings are telling and they will tell you where you are in your struggle. Take the censor off and let your feelings come out however they need to so infertility doesn't kill your soul, your dreams, or your ambitions. If you feel like you need to reroute your path to withstand this storm, then do that. This is your storm. Grab an umbrella, a raincoat, maybe some snow boots, gloves, perhaps some waders, whatever it takes... get prepared because you have a choice to make; you can choose to let infertility define you or you can defy it.

~

What does it mean to process that infertility is in your life?

It means asking some serious questions and taking time to answer them.
Can I live my life without kids?
Can I love my partner and my partner love me if we don't have kids?
Can I be in a relationship without kids... ever?
Am I enough and if not, why am I not enough?
Am I unlovable if I can't have children?
Am I mad because I just want to be mad at everything right now?
Am I blaming others to avoid my circumstance?
Do I feel rejected by my body?
Do I feel like less of a person?
What is my purpose if I'm not a parent?

Whatever your answers to the above are ok. If it is your truth, you need to own it. If you don't infertility will own you and sour your life like old garbage. I said it before and I will say it again: I will NOT sugarcoat this for you. I refuse to do that. I want to share honestly with you and to do that, I need to be truthful with you, your mind, and your heart, because you only get one life and it is begging you to live it.

This situation is bleak at best and going through the anger identifiers will get ugly but it is important to be honest, communicate clearly, and, when in doubt, apologize for sudden outbursts that may or may not hurt the feelings of others. NEVER apologize for your feelings. To be clear, I want to say this again to ensure you soak this piece in.

You need to own your feelings; doing this will help you understand your anger. When you're ready, you need to communicate them to yourself and those they affect; doing this will help you process your anger. Apologize to others if you hurt THEIR feelings; doing this will help you cope with anger. Do not apologize for YOUR feelings; doing this will help you love yourself past your pain. Make a commitment to the outcome you seek; doing this will allow you to be clear about your intentions around your anger.

~

There is no undo-redo button in life and, unfortunately, you can't undo this. Accepting this as your path and owning this as a part of your story, not a side effect anyone could have predicted, planned for, or deserved, is the only thing that will help you process anger. This is your life. Whether the infertility spawns from your side of the vagina or penis, it is imperative this not become a blame-game. Blame solves nothing and only generates more anger. This is someone's genetic make-up and to judge that means:

A.) you do not love them, which could very well be true,

B.) you do not know what Love is, which could also be true and

C.) you're basically really shitty, so you're fucked!

You can't truly love someone or yourself if that love comes with contingencies or blame. You are more than just an infertile person and, while you find it hard to see now, you will come to value yourself as a whole person and less as "infertile" through this process. If you're with someone who makes you feel inadequate, you need to speak with him or her about how they make you feel. Shoving shit under the rug at this stage is not something you should be doing to face your fears, feelings, and heal yourself.

You need to focus on what it is that that you want and if it is acceptance and understanding, then you can't hold back your truth. In doing this, you will arrive in a place that allows you to speak about infertility, not just to those going through it, but to anyone, and without falling into a weeping puddle on the floor. You will come to understand that when people make grandstanding comments about your infertility they're doing it to make themselves comfortable and it really has nothing to do with you but we'll talk more about this in stage three.

Identifying and then processing anger is a bridge to healing but you have to take steps in that direction before you can arrive there. Ultimately, if you're reading this, chances are you have already identified your infertility and it was shocking. Being mindful of your feelings about it as well as your partners is a must and being considerate of each other means being extremely cautious NOT to dwindle each other's existence down to sperm and eggs. It also means being aware that you are not blaming Mom and Dad for genetics; they didn't get to pick them anymore than you did. And not thinking that somehow you won the infertility lottery and only you carry the burden.

Infertility is not happening to you. It is a part of you but it is not you. Similarly, it is NOT your partner. There is no one to blame or carry this burden. You must reconnect to the part of you that is willing to accept you, or them, as more than this disease and let it grow to outshine your pain. You must choose your choice to minimize yourself into believing you are the victim or accept that you are more than this. There is always a choice.

When you begin to understand your anger about infertility, you will begin to understand your value in the world, in the lives of others, and, more importantly, what you feel about it yourself. Understanding is the mutual point at the Bermuda Triangle where anger, love, and choice meet. Anger is a powerful emotion because it shows us what we care about.

Yes. You want to have a baby.

Yes. It is painful to discover your body cannot do this thing you so desperately want it to do.

Yes. It is hard to accept that this is not the way you had imagined your life, but do not limit your value to this.

In evaluating anger, we make a choice to understand our priorities and what we need to be happy. This part of your journey will force you to evaluate the trajectory of your life by analyzing what you value and what those values mean to your existence. You will take time to understand what you can and cannot accept, ask yourself questions about what drives your anger, stop making excuses for it (own it and what happiness means to you), and begin to build a connection from what you thought your life was going to be, and realize what it can become.

Focusing on the light in your life does not mean you're avoiding feelings of inadequacy, trauma, or sadness. It does not mean you're egocentric. It does not mean you're self-absorbed. It means you're saving your fucking life. It's going to be hard but look at this as a chance to write a new chapter in your life and make a choice to feel better than you do now.

Things may not have taken the path you thought they would and it is really hard, but giving up is not a solution. It's quitting and committing to the idea that your life is not worthy of happiness and that is bullshit. Adapting is a part of life and it doesn't involve closing the book on happiness. You deserve to be happy and being sad, mad, or furious about that now does not take happiness away from you, but it is a telltale sign that you will need to work to find it. Yes. It will be scary, but life is scary anyway. At least with this you are going in search of the things that scare you with awareness.

Try to look at this as an opportunity to write your life as you want it and a chance to understand what being enough for yourself truly means. In the words of Bob Seger, "turn the page."

CHAPTER 9: DISCOVERING WHO YOU ARE IF YOU'RE NOT A PARENT.

L et's call it like it is; shock and anger are exhausting and by now, you are probably seeking calm. This isn't ridiculous. It's only logical to need a moment of release and reflection when you're everyday feels like the emotional equivalent of a dryer stuck on tumble.

Stop judging your emotions and start reflecting on them. It makes complete sense to ask you, "What the hell is happening to me?" Especially, if you're not sure how you got here, but you know that you don't feel like yourself anymore

Confusion in the midst of a life altering experience isn't unheard of or completely ridiculous. After all, I can get confused reading a recipe; so don't be too hard on yourself if you find you're getting tripped up in the throws of an emotional journey. Take a load off, and cut yourself some slack. It's not the worst thing in the world to unravel or pause and reflect. It is called being human and it's also called You Need To Take Freaking Care of Yourself.

Plainly stated, shock and anger can be vicious and also enlightening. If right now, you're emotionally exhausted, don't feel like yourself, don't trust your body, and not sure whose life you're in but you're very aware of how you feel and that is confused, desperate, and angry? Congratulations! This is fantastic self-awareness!

It might not feel fantastic. It may feel more like your life is a disaster, and less like progress, but at least you are aware.

If you are in a place where you have allowed yourself to be with your feelings around what you're going through, then congratulations are in order! You rode the rollercoaster like a champ! Take a moment of pause to celebrate because some people aren't willing to connect with their feelings about anything, let alone something as traumatic as infertility.

I know it seems ridiculous to celebrate acknowledging our rage but, again, if you feel something and clearly identify what it is, where it's coming from, and why it affects you, you are amazing!

In the realm of being a human, we have so many feelings in our arsenal that sometimes it is hard to identify what and why we're reacting a certain way. Therefore, choosing to experience an emotion and being able to understand it is an accomplishment. You chose to respond to your pain instead of avoid or deny it. Be proud of yourself.

~

By now, you have likely realized that each stage involves a continuation and reprocessing of the lessons and feelings mentioned before it. You may continue to process and reprocess what you think or feel throughout your journey. The great part about understanding your emotions is that once you go through them and allow yourself to feel it, getting through them in the future can become easier. It's like building a muscle. You become stronger, more flexible, and learn how to recover the more you work it. Once you build it, you can continue to increase strength or the use of it can become further developed and even improved.

The next stage in understanding where you are and what you are going through and how you may or may not be dealing with it doesn't imply you're done with anger or shock or denial. Or, that how you progress through any of the stages is linear. No. It means healing, just like feelings, can experience an overlap and residual effects can surface or linger. Consider yourself a human earthquake with emotional aftershocks.

You can't predict the outcome to any particular situation but it is possible you may have feelings about it. Point is, as you make your way through each stage, you may begin to see an overlap and, in some cases, how each contributes to those before, during and even after it.

Sorting through anger and bargaining is just like that. Anger can carry us a long distance, impacting everything in its path. Its force is strong. While bargaining is a tool we use to pretend it's not there or convince ourselves that we can make it go away. However, if we can pinpoint what encourages negative feelings and how to deal and heal them, then we might be able to assess what is behind it, how we're using it, how it's using us, and what we are or are not getting out of it.

You may be thinking, "I know why I'm angry. It's because I'm infertile or struggling with infertility."

I will challenge this thought. Infertility may be the cause of your anger, but what is driving it? What is giving infertility the power to make you emotionally charged?

When we refuse to acknowledge anger, it becomes a ticking time bomb that eventually, blows-up, harming all unsuspecting persons in its way. That includes you.

There is no way to prevent anger from showing-up. It's like a pimple. It is unpredictable, sporadic, and sometimes it really fucking hurts. Sometimes it goes away on it's own, and others we need to face it and intentionally, take it out. It's not something that will leave you, never to be heard from again.

Anger is a part of being a human. However, strengthening the awareness we have about how we express it and feel it can be managed by discovering where it lives .

~

What happens next is a combination of anger through depression, and bargaining through sadness. I want to be very clear here and state that when I speak of my infertility depression, I am not talking about it or sadness from a clinical perspective. I was not clinically diagnosed, with depression so I have neither professional assessment nor judgment about anyone who lives with and thrives through it.

Depression is important to me that in that I feel it is very highly judged and under emphasized. Therefore, it is beyond necessary that I point it out.

Depression is serious and if you feel perpetual sadness, please consider a clinical diagnosis. Help is available. It is there for you. Please allow yourself to receive it. If you feel the need to seek counseling, I strongly do recommend you do so.

When I refer to depression in this book, I am pointing to my self-diagnosed and elongated period of melancholy. A period of my life where I felt like I didn't know who I was anymore but more than that I didn't know how to find me.

I was so lost and so lost in my sadness that it went on for hours, days, months, and years. It lived within me and while I longed for the ability to have a genuine laugh, feel light and find joy, no matter what I did, I felt like it eluded me. I felt like it was no longer available to me. I felt like I couldn't see the value in life and if I couldn't find it, then it wouldn't find me.

Infertility can be exhausting. It will give you all the feels and sometimes many complicated ones. There is no shortcut.

Here is where you accept your feelings and also discover your proverbial exit or your Om. This is where you take on a fight or flight mentality. This is where the boys become Men. (It just seemed to fit there, ladies.) This is where you become so overwhelmed by trying to understand who you are now that infertility is in your life that it can become suffocating, isolating, and you guessed it, depressing.

I wish I could say that this next phase will be the most challenging, but hell it is all challenging. However, you are likely to experience feelings of anger, confusion, and exhaustion. It is important to recognize where you are emotionally as anger can drive you right into depression, which can cause you to think illogical things, like:

I'm ugly. I have no business having a baby anyway.
I'm not smart enough to have a child.
I'm not worthy of being a Mother.
I should just give-up on life, if I can't have a family.

Being ugly, stupid, and unworthy has zero to do with having a child. The only reason these and other useless thoughts pop into your head is because you are sad, fed-up, or even depressed.

Thinking this way is not helpful and will only hold you hostage from healing, and increase the likelihood to see your life as unlivable. This is bargaining.

~

Bargaining is your offering to the universe, God, Mother Nature, your uterus, penis or Peanut M&M's. This is the stage of infertility where you find yourself saying things like,

> This is happening to me because I'm a bad person.
> This is happening to me because I picked on my little brother growing up.
> This is happening to me because the Universe thinks I wouldn't be a good Mom.
> This is happening to me because God doesn't think I'm unworthy.
> This is happening to me because I don't go to church.
> This is happening to me as a sign I'm in the wrong relationship.
> This is happening to me because I'm not married.
> All of the above are examples of anger with bargaining.

For example, "This is happening to me because I'm not married." If you find yourself bargaining with this, perhaps issues of anger exist in your relationship. You may be well aware of these feelings or not. Either way, the underlying anger you have about your relationship could be the result of mixed feelings around it. These feelings may revolve around the level of commitment you feel from the person you're with but are more likely related to the uncertainty you feel about the relationship or feelings about who you are or are not being in it.

Breaking this down further:

Maybe, you want to be married but your partner doesn't.

Maybe, you don't want to be married but your partner does.

Maybe, both of you are happily unmarried but there's external pressure. (Coughs – Family!)

In any scenario, your relationship status has nothing to do with infertility or family.

Relationships and their status are primarily about the people in them. Some may argue that your family can affect your relationship. If that is your truth, then my only piece of advice is to bring a notepad and pencil to every conversation because there's bound to be many opinions.

If not, and you and your partner have enough to deal with, then this actually makes things a lot easier. See, progress already! Point is being angry at your relationship or in your relationship is not due to infertility. It can be a part of it, but chances are it is not the root cause of your problems.

Having a baby is stressful whether you are infertile or not. The anger you have about infertility may cause you to project feelings into directions that do not deserve blame. If you are feeling unfulfilled with your relationship, you need to speak with your partner. Or, if you live in the land of polygamy, then perhaps this discussion will involve multiple partners... like I said, notepad and pencil. Whatever your scenario, before you start a conversation that could potentially tailspin into a direction unintended, think long and hard about whether or not this is actually about your relationship.

For example, if you currently believe you are infertile because you aren't married. Bargaining comes into play in the form of blaming this for that. If you are doing this, it means you're willing to blame your relationship status for why you have not conceived. Basically, you're offering up marriage to the universe as a bargaining chip to have a baby.

Think about that for a second: you're not pregnant because you're not married? Hello, McFly! Never in the history of penises and vaginas has NOT being married ever stopped a sperm and egg. Look, I'm not trying to minimize this but I do want to be clear. In the land of infertility, if your moral, mental, and emotional compass points you in a direction that casts blame then you are bargaining. And, I'm no couple's counselor, but if you're willing to link your relationship to your misery, infertile or not, that says something about the relationship, and not the lack of a baby. Capeesh?

~

Anger and bargaining are sad. I know it. I cannot tell you how many times I bartered with myself during our struggle.

I gave up my daily exercises because I was told aggressive exercise can have a negative impact on your hormones while trying to get pregnant so I eliminated something from my daily routine that gave me great joy and a boost of self-esteem, in exchange for what I believed would help me improve my hormone levels and get pregnant.

I stopped dying my hair because the infertility drugs were making it frail and, as a result, it was having a negative reaction to bleach and falling out. Despite the fact that my hair is "my thing", I gave up on vanity and feeling beautiful, to continue with the fertility drugs, which I believed would help get me pregnant.

I quit going out because it costs a fortune to combat infertility, so I gave-up socializing with friends and any potential opportunity I had to get out of my infertility bubble to save money, so I could invest in fertility treatments to help me get pregnant.

Exercise, hair therapy, and having cocktails with friends may seem minimal to you but, for someone who found enjoyment and identity in all three, removing them from my life was a bad decision. Each of these gave me an outlet, a release, and interjected fun into an otherwise isolating, scary, and aggressive situation. I don't regret pursuing fertility treatments, but I do regret seeing the scenario as a one or the other choice. It didn't have to be choosing for me versus things that could get me pregnant. I chose that, because I thought I had to. I chose to bargain with my well-being.

Together anger and bargaining can take you to a place where you're willing to leverage all that makes you happy or content and exchange them for a baby. Man, is that some shit. Typing it aches my heart, and I desperately do not want that for you. Also, because it shows me how little I valued myself and the agony I was willing to endure for a baby.

If you don't like the word bargaining, consider sacrifice. Sacrifice is not a foreign idea when it comes to infertility. In fact, a lot of infertility is about making sacrifice for a new existence, ideally, one that involves a baby. However, when the path to your ideal existence becomes hard, long, and unfulfilling, that is when those sacrifices become punishing.

Sacrifice is not a foreign concept in life. I'm not suggesting that sacrifices are only difficult when endured alongside infertility. I am suggesting that when faced with a trauma, those little things that give you joy become much more than jumping jacks, root touch-ups, and Cosmopolitans. They become a release. They become self-nourishment. They become a lifeline to a reality that can save you from being a recluse, hating yourself, or worse.

The sacrifices made with infertility are in an effort to achieve a dream or an ideal reality. When you feel all the effort is in vain and due to a disease you didn't ask for, it's like someone set a bomb-off inside your life, so leveraging everything to happy becomes the next natural step.

175

~

As mentioned in stage one, you are more than just a vessel. You are a whole, magical, and beautiful person. In order to be of value to anyone else, let alone a baby, we need to have a complete understanding of our value. That means knowing who we are in this world. I'm not talking about Jane Doe, daughter of John and Janie Doe, sister to Jim-Bob and Jordan. I'm talking about who the fuck are you?

What makes you happy – assuming you can push infertility out of your mind for 5 minutes to actually confirm this? You are not infertility.

What is your S.S.B.? COME ON PEOPLE, that is a *Sex and the City* reference. S.S.B. is your "secret single behavior", the behavior you love to do when alone and used to do all the time while you were single. That shit defines you.

Why are you a good person? Truthfully, there is something. Stop thinking there isn't.

In what way do you add value to the world? Deep. Yes. Nothing is more enlightening than realizing your purpose or seeing that you live each day like Groundhog Day.

We all have a purpose. Wanting to have a child is beautiful. I want that too, but to envision it as your whole purpose means you don't know yourself very well nor do you value your life's potential.

To believe you are defined by your ability to have children means you do not value yourself. It can be a value add to one's existence, but it is not all we are. I can feel the ridicule and judgmental energy as I type this, but I believe it to be true. Your ability or lack thereof to procreate does not define you. It never did.

No movie, doctor, or book about children enhancing our lives should be manipulated or used as punishment to support the thoughts telling you that you're worthless without a family either. That's just mind games and storytelling. This also applies to religion.

If your religion has convinced you that your lot in life is to bear children, then what does that make you, my friend, now that you're infertile? A reject? A throw away human? Feel free to say, "Fuck That!." with me.

Don't get on your high horse. This is not to cast dispersions over religion or self-worth. However, this is to affirm that you are more than just a vessel. You are more than just an incubator. You are more than just a penis, vagina, one ovary, low sperm, or barren.

You are a person who has a soul, who loves, hurts, and generates feeling. You are not minimized by your inability to have children unless you make that choice for yourself. You can if you like. I'm not judging you. I made that choice everyday for 4+ years until I realized it wasn't what I wanted.

What I wanted was a life less ordinary. I wanted more than feeling like my story was the summary of doctors visits, blood samples, fertility meds, timed sexual encounters, failed pregnancies and questioning will I get my period this month? Four years of this on repeat was not what I wanted for me.

I wanted to feel alive and not like a useless, broken, lifeless, sad, lonely, and enraged piece of shit anymore. This may not be the way it is for you, but it is how it became for me, and I had to make it stop.

Tough Love: if you don't know who you are, you are wasting your life. Being unaware of what makes you tick is a telling sign. If you don't know, it's time to figure it out and below are a few helpful questions to get you started.

What do you love? This can be anything, people, places, or cheese.
What do you hate? This can be anything, people, places, or pleasantries.
What makes you laugh? This can be anything, people, places, or dry humor.
What do you enjoy doing? This can be anything, people, places, or Yoga.
Who do you enjoy doing it with? This can be anything, my husband, places, or things (switched it up!).
Why do you enjoy it? This can be anything, people, places, or things that keep me sane.
Where do you enjoy doing it? This can be anywhere, beaches, parks, or even your own backyard.
And, could you enjoy it on your own? Sorry. This is a yes or no. It is what it is.

These are all starter questions to help you pinpoint how you feel. However, the million-dollar question and answer about your infertility comes down to you. I wish I could tell you it's situational or something you can work through with your partner but that would be a lie. Finding your value in life will not come from a self-help book anymore than it will come from the opinions of your mate or bargaining pieces of your happiness away to the universe as trade.

Truthfully, you will have your own sobering response to what makes you happy or sad but be mindful of one very important detail: there is no wrong answer. Still, I will warn you that your response to life and what gives you satisfaction or not, much like infertility, can change many times and things about you or your relationships so be prepared. We'll talk more about how to be mindful of your relationship, maintain value for your individuality and stop yourself from unintentionally bargaining relationships in a jiffy, so hang tight.

~

Before I lay down the hammer on what I believe may be the most important question to ask yourself on your journey, I want to share a poignant quote that helped me navigate my healing process.

"If I asked you to name all the things you love, how long would it take for you to name yourself?" - unknown

I love this quote. More importantly, I value its sentiment, because with infertility, we can become hyper focused on a result: get pregnant. In pursuit of pregnancy, we can neglect our well-being. How we feel physically, mentally and emotionally becomes an afterthought. Ultimately, we overlook self-care in search of the goal.

Only you can know if you're treating yourself well and this brings us to the BIG question: can you be happy if you never become a parent?

As people, we often focus on things to make us happy and to those we assign meaning. Take for instance, infertility. For purposes of this example, I will assert that you were happy prior to discovering challenges with fertility. However, after the discovery, somewhere the focus shifted from I am happy and want to have a baby, to having a baby will make me happy.

This thinking isn't isolated to babies and infertility. It applies to everything. Whether it's thinking a baby, car, house, new job, or more money, will make you happy, it's all the same. It puts the responsibility for happiness out there in the world and waits for it to show-up. It takes all the power you have for achieving and sustaining happiness, and places it with something or someone else.

Waiting for it is what leaves you thinking, "If I get pregnant, I will find happiness."
Or, "If I get the raise, then I can be celebrate my accomplishments."
Or, "If I can afford that type of car or priced house, then I know I've made it."

This thinking takes our success, love, or happiness from being something we are accountable and responsible for, and makes the determination externally driven by what we are able to achieve. Whether it's the car, the house, or the baby, they all become responsible for your well-being, instead of you deciding I am successful or happy no matter what happens.

Yes. I lived with a, "If I get pregnant, I will find happiness" mindset for 4+years but it did nothing to bring me fulfillment.

Yes. Having a family may give you happiness but it is not responsible for sustaining it.

You are responsible for your happiness, without or without infertility, but you always were. Going through infertility didn't change that but your mind did.

Please don't misunderstand. I would like to have a baby too, and I know without a shadow of a doubt that it would make me happy, but going through infertility doesn't change whether or not I can still choose to live an amazing existence. It doesn't mean that if I never have a child I can't still feel fulfilled. I certainly can, but I, and you, will need to choose it.

For me, infertility changed the way I looked at what I needed to be happy. Everything that brought me joy got wrapped up in being a Mom and birthing a life. It changed how I saw happiness. It took me from thinking, "Being a Mother will bring me so much joy" to "I cannot have joy if I am not a Mother." It changed how I chose to access pleasure. It changed who I was, how I saw myself, and how I saw life. It took me from feeling like I was making a choice to produce life to I had no choice and no life, but that isn't true. It wasn't then and it isn't now. Let's look at an example.

For example, reading. NOTE: I realize reading and having a baby are not the same and do not have the same impact on one's happiness. This is an example so chill and stay with me for a moment.

Let's take for instance someone who says reading makes me happy. Well, I don't entirely agree. Reading does not make you happy. What you are reading, when you are reading it, and why you are reading it is what gives you joy.

The author does not give you pleasure. Not unless you know them personally, in which case, that's a different story - pun intended. The book does not give you meaning. You assign meaning based-on your response to the literature.

Think about it: how many books have you picked-up, thought this blows, and it's now a permanent coaster on your nightstand? The book went unfinished because you found its content boring. Therefore, reading does not make you happy. The literature you choose, the meaning you assign the words within it, and enjoying what you like about it is what makes you happy. The same is true for having a baby.

Having a child will not make you happy. The meaning you assign to the love and act of parenting is likely what you are after. Infertility is a hard road to travel because it forces you to understand your desire for a child beyond "I want a baby". It makes you look in depth at the why and evaluate if a baby is nonnegotiable. If it is, there are many routes you can take to become a parent but we'll get into that much later.

If you are in a place where you find yourself resting your happiness on a baby, and contemplating if you are enough, I would suggest that now is a great time to uncover what's responsible for your joy and if it includes just being you? Beyond that, it might be great time to check-in with your partner about how you're feeling, how the struggle is affecting your happiness, and how this is affecting you together. To take it a step further, you might also want to chat about your relationship and if it can sustain itself without a child. Once you understand what gives you joy, you can truly understand how this impacts you, your relationship and the future.

A great way to determine your level of happiness is to come-up with 5-10 reasons why, if you weren't you, you would be your own Best Friend. Seriously. Sit and jot down why you are the bee's knees because you are!

Once you confirm that you are equally as awesome as Lady Gaga, then you can begin to understand why having a baby only adds value to your life and is not the sole reason your life is of any value. Point is when you diminish your worth to breeder, and you undervalue your life, if you're not careful, this type of behavior is not only crippling to you but also to the people you care about.

If you're like me, you've spent the better part of your 20's trying not to get pregnant. Sorry, Mom and Dad. Meanwhile, now you are "Infertile Myrtle" and you don't know how to feel. Again, let me be the first to confirm it is totally back-ass-wards but being fucked-off about it won't change that there are people out there getting pregnant without trying and you can't. Therefore, it's time to stop playing the avoidance game and assess how in the hell you are doing right now and face the truth.

How does not knowing your "Infertile Myrtle" self affect your life?
For starters, it makes you sad and that's okay.

It's more than undesirable to feel as if your body is out to get you. It's not true but, if telling yourself that makes you feel better, it's fine to hold onto it for the next two seconds. Yes. Two seconds is all you get because it's a LIE.

It is totally fucked that other ovaries or sperms in the world seemingly work great and yours is broken. Again, not true. Your pieces and parts are not broken; they just can't create a baby on their own.

It is justified to feel anger when people who do horrible things have babies. The world is a fucked-up place, no sense focusing energy on shit you can't change when you're trying to tackle your own shit.

It is okay to feel jealous and secretly roll your eyes when you see the 9 millionth Facebook post of "my baby is the size of an eggplant". Roll your eyes at home, not to people's faces. There's no good that can come from becoming the "Mean Infertile Myrtle".

Being unhappy with your life does not mean you can't celebrate others wins or their babies. Transversely, it doesn't mean you can't be sad about this for yourself but you need to find a way to push through thoughts of "Why is this happening to me" and accept;
1. It is not you – see stage two – it is happening to you.
2. And, while it is happening to you, it's not who you are.
3. And, while it's not who you are, it is not other people either.

Moral, don't bring down the negativity hammer on others and ruin their happy, only to make you look like a heartless human who is incapable of celebrating victories for others when they are deserved. That is not who you are and I am confident, it is not who you want to be. You need to find a way to be happy for other people and in a way that doesn't involve anger and bargaining.

Let's make a little Lord of the Rings reference, shall we? Remember how Gollum became obsessed with the gold ring? Well, let me show you a mirror my friend because right now you're bald, stressed out, and wearing a loin cloth threatening to kill people over a piece of jewelry, "my Precious!" Except, you are not a Hobbit, you are you, and you are not coveting a ring, you are coveting pregnancy and, might I add, happiness in general.

When we're sad, sometimes we can't see that it affects how we show-up in the world . In an effort to protect our internal hurt, we also cannot see how this causes us to over emphasize our behavior. At our saddest, being happy for someone else can be a chore and, in an effort to force the appearance of a genuine happy emotion, sometimes we don't see that our being can overtake a moment.

When we become ridden with emotion, sometimes we covet all good and bad things because we don't have harmony in ourselves. We absorb an idea that no one could possibly understand how we feel and, even if we told him or her, they still wouldn't know. Well, I'm here to tell you that is partially true.

You can explain your situation to people 1,000 times over and they still won't feel how you yearn for a positive pregnancy test, nor the knot in your throat each time you discover someone else is pregnant. However, that doesn't mean you get to covet emotion or struggle.

People go through struggle. They may not go through the same struggle as you, but believe me they go through bad shit! You cannot over exaggerate your appearance of happiness and expect people to know that inside you are dying in a cesspool of infertility misery. Conversely, do not risk your relationships with others by refusing to share how you feel if it is YOU who will not let them in.

More Tough Love: pregnancy is not yours to covet. It is beyond a measurable doubt that this is probably the saddest you've ever been in your life. However, you do not own a corner share on the infertility market. Therefore, you cannot make your infertility depression overshadow all elements of life. This includes relationships.

For instance, the unavoidable Baby Shower Party. If you are secluding yourself from Baby Showers because you are afraid you will turn into a wailing mess in the middle of the 15th box of Pampers? DO NOT GO. But you know what else you DON'T do? You do not skip-out on the shower and weeks later explain to your very dear friend why you didn't go.

If you feel something, honor it. Also, if you feel uncomfortable attending, then you need to take responsibility for it. You need to have the awkward conversation and expect that your friend will understand. And, if she doesn't understand, you can be sorry for your friends hurt feelings but you are not responsible for them any more than she is for yours.

Speak your truth and own it. Do not victimize yourself by avoiding uncomfortable truths especially if you are not in a place where you've opened up about how this is affecting you.

Infertility can be a big black cloud that follows you if you let it. Do not let it fog your judgment and ability to care for those who you love and love you.

Do not allow it to become the wedge between you and an opportunity for others support you. Do not let it make you feel alone.

Remember, bargaining is when we behave a certain way and use the outcome as a reason for why we're doing it. It is when we offer up something in exchange for what we want. Basically, don't offer-up important relationships to the universe and use infertility as a reason for why you get to be the victim. ICK! That ain't pretty.

In order to stop being Gollum, you need some release. You have to share your journey with someone and stop acting like it's better for anyone that you pretend this isn't happening.

~

Remember when I told you, we'd talk more about how you prepare yourself to be mindful of your relationship, maintain value for your individuality, and stop yourself from unintentionally bargaining relationships in a jiffy so hang tight? Well, I'm no liar, so away we go!

I want to say upfront, that this is big and important.. The relationships you have in your life are and should be impactful to who you are as a person. It is vital that you own your individual value but it is equally as important that you care for those around you because these are the people who either wiped your ass when you couldn't or will be there to wipe it later. HANDLE WITH CARE.

For now, I'll lead with this sentiment; if you are in a relationship with someone you love and who loves you and you are both on this infertility rollercoaster together, then that tells me something important. At some point, you knew your value enough to choose a person who values you. Or, you had parental units that taught you how to value yourself and thus, you chose someone who could handle the job. That being said, the most dangerous thing we can do through our struggle with infertility is close off. Not just because it can stunt your ability to heal but also because it can ruin your relationships.

If you are in a committed relationship, then you have a responsibility to continue to nurture that connection for as long as you are committed. No amount of pain or grief is an excuse to shut the door on people you love.

Here are a few ways to be mindful of your relationships. Talk. Say the words people. I was terrible at this.

I, a Communications Major, did relatively zero communicating with anyone. This did not serve me well and I tend to think it may have contributed to why it took me years to have a genuine happy emotion again. I wasn't talking to anyone. I was staying inside my head. I was simmering in my negativity and had nothing to break-up the self-deprecation. Point is no one knows what you're going through unless you verbalize it. Sometimes talking through things helps us to understand ourselves but, more importantly, it allows those in your life to feel connected to you.

Allow people to have feelings.
If you're upset about infertility, chances are your partner is upset about it too or upset about it for you. Do not discount empathy. Processing infertility is overwhelming. You may feel like you have enough on your plate and that you can't handle your partner's grief too but give talking a chance. You may find that a doorway of relief is opened in having someone to share your feelings with and to commiserate in the difficulty of the experience.

Do not victimize yourself.
Having a feeling and working through it is one thing but having a feeling and pushing others away does not make people feel bad for you or want to be around you. When we share ourselves, people feel connected to us. When we close off, well, don't be surprised if no one comes to your rescue when you need them. The people in your life cannot connect with someone who doesn't want to be connected to. Have you ever tried walking through a locked door? Yeah. It's really freaking hard to break-in and get through, unless you have been invited or have the key. Closing off is all kinds of bad for your relationship mojo. You must do your best to see yourself as a "work in progress" and not a "lost cause". If you decide to be in accessible, then don't be shocked when no one can reach you.

Apologize for sudden outbursts or unintentionally, hurting people.
It is not okay to assume that because you are "going through something" this gives you a right of passage to treat people like shit. You can be as emotional as you want but you are still expected to treat others like they are humans with emotions too. Being mean just makes you mean. It doesn't make you mean BECAUSE he or she is struggling with infertility. No Excuses.

Do not apologize for your feelings.
I've said this before and I'll say it again. You should acknowledge that people have feelings and appreciate their feelings. However, if you do not agree and you legitimately, in your bones, feel something DO NOT APOLOGIZE FOR IT. This includes I have infertility and right now I need to be alone as well as I don't like raisins so I won't eat them. Do not apologize for that, shit. Own your feelings and stand-up for them. Those who love you will respect your space and what you need. Those who don't? Well, bye.

Do not concoct arguments or assume someone's intention.
In emotional times, we can become uber sensitive. It is important to become your own devil's advocate and try your best to ask yourself, "Is my husband being a dick right now? Or, am I on the edge and ANYTHING he said would piss me off?" If the answer is yes, tell your person, "Hey, you're being a dick right now" but also that you're feeling like a Tasmanian devil in a cage and not to take personally the shit flying out of your mouth. It is a fair warning and let's others know that today is a bad day. Everyone has bad days.

Own your responsibility to each situation.
If you do freak-out, say you are sorry! It's one thing to remind someone of his or her responsibility, it's another to freak-out over something that isn't dire or urgent. If you explode then you need to apologize.

Do not pretend you are the only person to go experience a tough time.

If you're mad, fine, be mad but do not project it. #8 goes hand in hand with #3. If you are distraught that's okay. People understand distraught. What people do not understand is victimizing one's self and seclusion. No one, not even the person who loves you the most in this world, which mind you, should be you, wants to be around someone who is a loose canon. After all, think about how hard it is to be in your own thoughts everyday. Now think about being someone who is trying to steer the unpredictability of living with you. Yeah. That's like trying to tiptoe through a field with land mines. You can have compassion for people who have been in your scenario before, because you relate to them. That makes sense. But, do not forget to have compassion for those who have NOT been in your situation before. You are both trying your best to understand a new and unpredictable situation. You might as well try to route the tough times together. Who knows, it might even make the relationship stronger? Communicate with your people.

Allow yourself as much time as you need to process your situation.

"Are we there yet?" Ugh. How annoying is that? It's pretty fucking annoying. Do not allow any preconceived notions about time conflict with your ability to process how you feel. There is no amount of time involved in processing emotions. However, you must communicate to your partner where you are if you need to think or aren't able to process things. If you feel like you're alone on an island without Tom Hanks and Wilson, then you need to say the words. Your person will never be able to understand the depths of your feelings if you do not share them. In sharing, they will be able to travel this process with you and, perhaps, understand where you are and maybe help you. Point is if you need time to have all the feels it is allowed but you need to level set with people and tell them.

Grieving does not need to be done alone. You are not alone.

There is no expiration date on grief. It can come and go and years later show up on your doorstep with luggage. Grief takes time and some moments will require deep thought, which may feel more comfortable dissecting alone. However, if and when the day comes where you need a hug in the middle of the afternoon because you are feeling especially vulnerable, go get that hug. Chances are your partner needs it too. In any relationship, we're generally tuned-in to our "people. Without saying anything, they are painfully aware you're grieving and know they cannot take that pain away. All they can do is love you and support you. It is your duty, yes, it is an actual responsibility you must take and do if you value relationships, to get to a place where you allow them to be there for you. Also, you must allow them to grieve too. Unsurprisingly, there is no time continuum on their grief either. This is not a one-sided process. We, you and your partner, both need to say the words, communicate your feelings, and work this shit out together or else. Well, or else you run the risk of losing each other. After all, what is the point of a relationship if not to allow each other to be human, have emotions, and be there for each other? This is called nurturing and if you take that away what is left?

Being unhappy with yourself doesn't mean you're unhappy in life. Just because you struggle to understand fallopian tubes, motility, and endometrium, doesn't mean everything in your life has to change. Let us not become so self-absorbed in our trauma that we forget it is also tragic for those who love us. Do not let them feel alone and do not let them make you that way either.

It's a complicated seesaw but this is what you sign-up for in relationships: the good and the bad. No one ever got an award for surviving a struggle on his or her own. Allow your persons to fulfill their duty in being there for you and in allowing, whether you see it or not, you are being there for them too.

~

You are more than just a vessel. Remember? You are a person, a whole person, with all kinds of complicated feelings that accompany the easy and life altering situations much like the one you're in. However, if it is not already apparent to you, you have always been more than someone's Mom or parent.

I want you to take a breath because this next part is deep.

Being a mother, father, or parent is a beautiful thing. I am lucky enough to have two amazing parents who taught me the value of being vulnerable and strong. To me, that is what a parent does.

A parent is someone who teaches others to be strong, to love, to believe in their self-worth, to help when it is needed and not, and to encourage others to know that having a tough time is a part of this thing called life.

Both of my parents ingrained in me that I was strong so when I was diagnosed with infertility what is the first thing I did? I forgot I was strong. Go figure. Who was the first person to notice that I forgot? My mom.

I love my mom, gosh, almost more than I love myself. She is the reason I am writing this to you. She is the reason I believe that we are more than just penises or vagina's destined to be the birthing unit of more penises or vaginas. She's the best fucking person I know in the world and she has always been so much more to me than just my mom.

Even though my mom has always said she is not my "friend", she has been the best non-friend I've ever had. She was there for me during all my fits of rage, incoherence, and insanity, which was impressive because I wasn't actually saying anything about how I felt. I was just taking it out on her and she never once judged me for it. She took it, all of it, both when I was freaking out and when I was pushing her away.

She is my mom. She knew I was in pain and she took it all like the fucking badass she is. She watched lovingly as my hair fell out after hormones took their toll on me and told me I was beautiful. She held my hand as the doctors wheeled me into surgery and, without one single tear, confidently said, "You got this" because, even if I didn't know it then, she was right. She knew I would be okay because she is more than just a mom who knows her kid. She is a wonderful person.

For most of you, in this moment, being a Mom or Dad means having a positive pregnancy test. Being a Mom or Dad means telling friends and family we're pregnant and them being so excited! It means watching bellies grow for 9 months and seeing what we look like with that belly or making emergency runs to the grocery story for ice cream at 2 AM. That is not a Mom or a Dad.

A Mom or a Dad is a contributor, an educator, a lover, a thought-provoker, a humanitarian, and a coach. They are someone who devotes their time and energy to making others know their worth and pushing that belief out into the universe as much and as often as possible, not only because it's true, but because the world needs it and it's the right fucking things to do.

You do not need to have perfect sperm or eggs to be a Mom or a Dad. You can be all those things and without squeezing anything out of an impossibly small hole.

I know. There is nothing I can do to calm your feelings of rage or anger and loss or grief but I hope you see that you are, and have always been, more than someone who is defined by their vagina, uterus, penis, scrotum, or any other anatomical part.

You don't need to minimize yourself to those things and you don't need to bargain with your life or the lives of those you love to feel a sense of value. You have always had the ability to be a contributor, an educator, a lover, a thought-provoker, a humanitarian, and a coach. From birth, you have always had the ability to be all those things and being a parent does not give you those qualities. You can live a perfectly full and wonderful life, even if your name is never Mom or Dad.

CHAPTER 10: GRIEVING YOUR FAIRYTALE.

Anger, like any blemish, is a nag. It takes stock of the negativity and uses it to keep us accountable to the way we live now and how those feelings can affect our future. However, thoughts of bargaining are counterintuitive to progress, no matter how negative it may feel, and keep us living in the past.

Bargaining isn't "wrong" but it is a tool we use to barter away the facts. Think about it this way. If you know something to be true, you cannot go back and reverse the information. Although, if you are bargaining,, you are missing a wonderful life.

Anger keeps you in tune with your feelings. Bargaining keeps you focused on what is driving those feelings. And, if anger says, 'I want a baby', while bargaining is saying, 'I'll exchange something for it and this whole mess will go away', then you're using anger and bargaining to live in the past and avoid truth.

When we barter with our relationships, we risk losing a potential lifelong commitment in hopes we can somehow correct the past. If we barter with our feelings, we risk those fulfilling relationships in hopes silence will make the situation obsolete. When dissected, anger and bargaining can be incredibly useful to understanding your pain and why you can't seem to break free of it.

Why do you stay mad?
Why can't you get out of bed in the morning?
Why do you feel worthless?
Why do you hate yourself?
Why do you hate the world?

Anger and bargaining help us to identify our mad behaviors so we can work on finding ways to heal them. As counteractive as they are, as unproductive as they seem, and as much as it will hurt like hell and feel like you're stuck in a dark abyss surrounded by negativity for a very long time, understanding these feelings will lead to a breakthrough. Anger and bargaining are your doorway to grief.

~

Listen, there is still a happily ever after in this scenario but it requires tweaking, reevaluating, and dealing with your shit. What it doesn't involve is a sweet old lady with a magical wand and a pink bubble that corrects your infertility and makes it all better.

That is not a story. This is a life. Fairytales are make-believe. You are real.

There is no way to negotiate or "Bippidi-Boppidi-Boo" your way out of hurting. There is no way to reverse the diagnosis. You are in the zone. You are working on yourself. You are in step four of five and, if you are putting in the work, you may even start to notice a difference.

Again, there are alternatives to having children, which we will discuss more in stage five, but before you apply your "Baby Band Aid" and skip straight to the end, give your grief the respect it deserves.

We touched on "Baby Band-Aids" in stage two and here they are again in bargaining and depression, rearing their baby Band-Aid heads.

In bargaining and depression, we tell ourselves, "If I get pregnant, then I will get out of this depression and be happy again." Hello, coulda...shoulda... and, woulda... not helpful!

It is not helpful to bargain with your life. It's not helpful to tell ourselves that a baby will make us happy. You need to make you happy and coulda, shoulda, and woulda-ing, all over yourself will only make a true mess of things.

When we're transitioning from anger and bargaining, to bargaining and grief, it's natural to feel confused. Remember, you are riding the emotional wave and spinning-out of control.

You are probably going to think some off-the wall shit, cast blame, have random outbursts, and run into seclusion. You may even revert backward in your feelings before you ever move forward. Whatever it is you do while transitioning into your grief, try not to use a baby Band-Aid to placate your pain.

A baby Band-Aid is a bad idea all the way around. Nothing can cure your hurt but you. Pain is a powerful, jealous, and all consuming. It demands to be felt but the power of now is just as strong. Living in the moment, accepting what is and finding a way to let in those scary feelings of grief, is what can help heal you.

What are some Baby Band-Aid Warning Signs?

"I'm fine." You cannot change your infertility diagnosis, anymore than you can change your anger about it. Avoiding your feelings does not do anything but keep you stuck. Process so you can progress.

"I blame my XYZ for this." No amount of blame can change what is. This isn't anyone's fault and, although it may not be what you envisioned, it is happening. No one can save you or change it for you so you need to find a way to live with it. Own it so it doesn't own you.

"Coulda...shoulda... woulda..." Living in the past and avoiding your reality is keeping you from processing how you feeling and moving forward. Heal so you can deal.

As people, we tend to be problem-solvers in a sense that we think from problem to solution. Meaning, we say, "Oh, there's a problem? Well, let's just find the solution and we'll make it all better." Listen, Bob the Builder, we're all very motivated by your "can-do attitude" and it's nice that you believe you can "fix it" but we need to make sure that the "fix" is transformational and not just... you guessed it, a band-aid.

Your struggle can be transformative! Transformational work is done with introspection, taking accountability, and examining the facts versus interpretations of a situation. It does not take into account what is fair or unfair. Unfortunately, there is no space for that in healing and I hate to have to be the one to tell you this, but fairness of a circumstance doesn't matter.

What matters is self-recognition. Who are you being about this situation,? How do you allow it to affect you? How does it impact who you are in the world? And, whether things workout in your favor or not, what do you really want to have happen in relationship to it?

Said another way, who are you now that infertility is in your life? How do you allow infertility to affect your thoughts, feelings, emotions, and actions? How does infertility impact your treatment of self and others? And, given all the facts that you have about infertility, if things workout the way you want them to or not, how do you want to live the rest of your life?

If infertility is causing a breakdown in the current version of your happily ever after story, know that I totally get that. If you are tired of feeling like it is a permanent breakdown, and I would assert you are because you're here with me, then it is time to do some transformation. It is time to go in search of healing. It is time go from breakdown to breakthrough.

~

Grief is not a feeling that we route by taking the HOV lane to *Pleasantville*. If it were, there'd be a lot les people crying at funerals.

When we come to terms with something, it is important it's well thought-out and something we can reuse in the event baby Band-Aids rear their little heads again. Transformation and healing will help you move your way in and out of grief.

Transformation and healing present themselves to us when we understand what it is we're dealing with,, upset about and willing to take accountability for . We forge ahead day after day, week after week, and, in some cases, year after year, driven by pain, guilt, and ego, all the while never truly understanding what it is we're grieving, why, nor evaluating the choices we've made that sustain our pain versus heal it.

There can be many causes for grief. It can be fear, worry, blame, resentment, or sorrow. The possibilities are endless. Ultimately, it is having awareness to it and understanding what our breakdown is around it that can gives us clarity.

I want to warn you. Yes. Another warning!

When you experience a breakthrough around grief, it can be surprising, emotional, and overwhelming, but as you process, grow, and emotions change so can how you manage it.

Grief and pain are not static emotions; just as you evolve, they do too. Just as you progress through your feelings, so will they. Just as you accept newness into your life, how you manage what you're dealing with will shift, perhaps grow strong, and, in some instances, fade. It is important to remember that as you process grief you allow it to be what it is and, in doing so, permit yourself to be malleable to it.

Grief Exercise: Write down your automatic and instinctive response.
Why are you angry?
What is causing you pain?
How are you enabling your pain?
What is your grief?
How are you giving grief space to be?
What is the grief giving you?
What will make you happy?
Why will this make you happy?
What is in the way of your happiness?
What will happiness make possible?

Let's try this again; I have listed possible answers to some of the questions to help you arrive at your own conclusion.

1. *Why are you angry?*
Possible Answer: People get pregnant who don't want babies. I want a baby and I can't.

2. *What is causing you pain?*
Possible Answer: I know my husband & I would be great parents. I'd love to have a piece of both of us walking around but I can't give that to him.

3. *How are you enabling your pain?*
By believing infertility is my fault.

4. *What is your grief?*
Possible Answer: I will never know how it feels to create & give life or meet that beautiful human who is both ½ him & ½ me.

5. *How are you giving grief space to be?*
I cry alone.

6. *What is the grief giving you?*
Grief gives me a space to unleash my anger, resentment, and sadness.

7. *What will make you happy?*
Possible Answer: Having a baby, being a Mom, & raising a person who is both ½ me and ½ my husband.

8. *Why will this make you happy?*
Possible Answer: Being a parent is one of life's greatest opportunities & I know my husband wants a baby.

9. What is in the way of your happiness?
Feeling like I'm a waste of a human who offers no value to my husband, my family, or myself. Me, basically, I am in the way of my happiness.

10. What will happiness make possible?
I can stop hating myself, have a great life, find joy again, and forgive myself.

The above exercise requires brutal honesty. You can answer it with whatever comes to mind, but to get anything out of it, I suggest you take time to be alone and search deep for a full response. It's likely you will unearth thoughts and emotions you have zero awareness about.

Try your best not to be too judgy about them. Let whatever comes up flow freely and without censorship, and notice what you uncover. After all, perspective is an amazing thing. Just by taking a moment to be with your feelings or to sit and consider them, you can gain immense clarity.

For instance, it took me four years to realize I was sad that I couldn't have a baby. Yup. That's it. You may be thinking, "well, duh, aren't we all?" But, I wasn't aware that for me, that was the bottom line. I wanted to. I couldn't. And, that rocked my world.

Sure. The sadness I felt was for a multitude of reasons but the number one reason I was sad, is because I couldn't have one.

It took me four years to conclude that I was pissed-off at society, women, penis's, vagina's, Mom, Dad, babies and the breeders who can procreate, because I could not. That's it. No great story about how I feel cheated which I did and still do. Short, sweet, and straight to the point.

I am fucking pissed off, because I fucking want to be a Mother. I can't, and that fucks me up all kinds of ways, because even those who don't want children can.

It makes me feel inadequate and guilty all at the same time. I want to have a child, and I can't; that is my grief in a nutshell.

Not only do I grieve because I can't do something but also because I feel guilt about the fact that I cannot do it. They're two halves of a whole.

It took me four years, countless tears, and several moments of silence to get to the bottom of my grief but I did it. You'll also probably notice I said that I feel cheated and still do.

Remember, you don't arrive at a conclusion of grief without some grand understanding of its driver. For me, my grief is that I feel guilt about not being able to be a Mom and my driver is that everyone else is doing it. I know. I KNOW. If everyone else jumped-off a bridge, would you? I mean... if you know me, then you know the answer to that question. YES! That sounds like an amazing time. Let's do it today! However, that's my grief driver. My driver is envy.

Like I said, understanding your grief is going to require that you get brutally honest with yourself because healing from it could mean admitting some unglamorous shit and to ingest that and "get over yourself" you will need to take a big spoonful of humble pie.

I understand your aversion to this. It's not glamorous to acknowledge what make us jealous. I don't even like pie and I just did it. You can do this and I suggest that you do for no other reason than it may help you too.

~

Accepting grief means being present to your present and nothing lays the foundation for emotional awareness like the light of day and realizing you have a slim chance of ever carrying a baby. It is like getting your ass kicked every .05 milliseconds. Once you accept this, reality can creep in super fast and before you know it, welcome to infertility depression!

From my experience, I'd compare depression to boxing. Except in this instance it is you against yourself. It is quick moving yet the beatings feel as if they're slow as molasses and never ending. There are ebbs and flows, jabs and hits, it stops and starts, and just when you think it's all over, it begins again.

Depression is not a sign of defeat. It can be, however, a sign that you are grieving a great loss.

I love you too much to let you sail-off into the sunset thinking the pain will just subside "someday", because someday will never come. You will continue to sit in a cesspool of your own misery until you realize you are choosing to beat yourself up. I know. I did this. For years, I sat in a place where I hated myself, my body, my life, my infertility depression, my happiness, everything. I hated everything.

How do I know I was experiencing depression with my infertility? How low was I? How terrible was my depression?

In the lowest of moments, I found myself sitting in a dark room on a random Saturday in November. It was about 1:30 PM. It was raining outside so it was a gloomy day. I hadn't moved from the same spot on our sofa for hours which means I was still in my pajamas and probably working some hair curling morning-to-afternoon breathe.

I was crying, but not just tears. I was sobbing in my grief and my depression was soaking it up like a sponge when my husband came down the steps and found me. He asked me what was wrong and what came out of my mouth next haunts me to this day.

I would use a word more profound than "haunts" but it swirls inside my head as a beaming reminder of just how depressed I was. What did I say? What became the shocking siren that made me painfully aware I was neck deep in a depression?

I said, "I know why people kill themselves."

Whew. Typing that makes my eyes well-up and gives me a moment of pause. It's not easy to admit I had lost myself.

I am not proud of this. I was not raised to be this person. My parents are great parents. They love me and this admission in no way reflects them.

I have an amazing family. I have an amazing husband. I even have a cat and dog who love the shit out of me and lick my face like it's a salt stick everyday, but I was so depressed I had began to have thoughts of suicide.

The day I told my husband, "I know why people kill themselves", was a very weird day for me. Hell, I'm sure that wasn't like Christmas morning for him either, but it was a strange moment.

For me, it was a day of reckoning. It was a day of eerie realization. It was a day where I had stopped questioning who I was and realized who I had become.

The minute I thought of suicide, I was scared. It's weird because I wasn't scared by the action of it. Rather, I was scared that my brain could even arrive at the idea. When I thought I didn't know who I was anymore, this jolted me into reality. I had become the girl who considers suicide and when that concept emerged I was overwhelmed.

Suicide and just the thought of it made me cry. I didn't just cry-cry, like watching a chick-flick or the moment in the Lion King where Mufasa dies and Simba walks over to him and says, "Dad, get up". I sobbed. I may have even wailed and pitched a bit of a fit.

The realization of who I was, and what my life had become, took everything out of me, and so all the hyperventilating; crying, erratic breathing, and uncontrollable bodily responses you can imagine, came with it.

I cried for all the things I didn't understand, the amount of time we had committed to this journey, and to the empowered part of me that I had silenced for so long; for all the emotions I kept buried, the pain and agony of facing every period as a defeat, and the girl inside of me who desperately wanted to stop feeling like a failure because she couldn't and possibly, wouldn't, ever conceive.

I didn't know what I wanted out of life. I didn't know who I was if I wasn't fighting for a baby. But, I knew I couldn't live like this, and the fact that the alternative, which presented itself to me was death... well, that scared me fucking shitless.

It makes me incredibly sad to know how far I fell in losing my value. I put myself in a really dark place, for a very long time, and I couldn't find myself. If that is where you are too, it is okay to feel sad about this. It is okay to grieve this but you MUST admit where you are with it.

I do not say this lightly. In fact, I say it with such delicate distinction because you need to know that you are more than your infertility and it has no right to make you feel like you have no value, but it can. I know it. I see you. I hear you. I've been there too.

If you're reading this and you feel like I did, I want to caution you to take it very seriously. Do not hesitate to call your local suicide hotline right away. Call 800-SUICIDE (800-784-2433); 800-273-TALK (800-273-8255); or, for the hotline for the hearing impaired, call 800-799-4889. Or contact a mental health professional as soon as possible.

I do not shy away from sharing this with you, in fact, part of the reason I wrote this book is because I needed to share this very specific piece with you. I do not wear my deep dark depression like a badge of honor but I do not wear it like a branding of embarrassment either.

For me, this part of my journey was a sign that I needed to do something different. This was a sign that I was choosing to lay down and die in my fight. In that moment, I kid you not, mere moments after I said this to my husband, I got up, got a shower, brushed my stinky teeth, and started researching what was happening to me and bought my very first personal development book on how to get my shit together. Thank you, Jen Sincero!

I am not telling you this so you feel bad for me. I am sharing it in hopes that you may identify your scenario or maybe even glimmers of your scenario within an example. I don't want to think about what happens when you succumb to the maniacal lows of a depression because without saying it we both know it can't be pretty and I was dangerously close.

If you hear or see something in this for you, please take a pause and realize that this isn't who you want to be. If you want to lie down and die, then that is up to you. THINK ABOUT THAT! Because it is fucking scary and it should sound fucking scary. If you DON'T want to lie down and die, then you need to get the fuck up, understand that being in a depression about your grief over a life you thought existed for you is completely understandable, and FIGHT! You are not infertility; you have a life that deserves to be lived. Get Up and Fight!

~

This fight isn't about Mom or Dad, or anything other than realizing your struggle is not the result of something "wrong" with you. It is the result of something affecting you. If you feel strongly about the grief of your infertility diagnosis and you feel strongly it has totally jacked-up the happily ever after you've been planning since playing Barbie's with Amy from down the street, then yes, it is completely acceptable to feel as if this situation is depressing you.

Who wouldn't be fucking sad to find out something that they've been planning isn't a possibility!? I was so sad and it made me feel depressed. The end.

Please don't allow yourself to get caught up on the societal shame of depression. Depression has a negative connotation because it is perceived as meaning something is wrong with you and you need to "fix that". No one has the right to judge you for feelings. There is no right way to feel.

If you are grieving and in that grief processing anger, shock, bargaining, and depression is just another stop along the way, then it's all a part of your process. Don't let anyone's judgments squelch what you are feeling.

Give your emotions space to be what they are and give yourself the love to be present and open to whatever comes up. It is acceptable to mourn the loss of a life that gave yours meaning by acknowledging it may never happen. It is more than okay to sit with your grief. Anyone who tells you, you shouldn't be upset over the loss of your fairytale can have his or her opinions. You just don't have to care about them more than your own.

~

One...
Managing your infertility depression can be about understanding your grief. For me, it was about understanding that I was grieving a fairytale. It never happened; it was all an idea.

Two...
There is no way for you to change that other people will continue to procreate and some with ease. For me, it was about understanding that this is not the universe's way of saying, "FUCK YOU". It is the facts of life.

Punch!

If you're going to grieve the pain, then you might want to consider that there is no way to grieve it without knowing a part of you will forever be changed by this experience. That's OK. Change can be good. It can be enlightening. It can be empowering. It can be transformative. Ultimately, you matter and you have a life worth living and it begins when you stop feeling sorry for yourself. I know hearing that is like taking a bullet but I wouldn't say it to you if I didn't also at one point in time have to say it to myself.

Top 5 signs you're grieving:
You are not talking to anyone about your feelings.
You are angry with other people for having babies.
You can't be happy for other's life "wins".
You find yourself wondering, "what did I do to deserve this"?
The resounding response you hear when thinking, how do I move on, is *I can't* or *I don't know?*

Feeling sad for a reason is completely different than feeling sad for no reason. What does that mean? It means that if you're sad and even though you feel like you don't know why, there is a reason. You just haven't got to the bottom of it yet.

Facing infertility depression over a life you wanted is "normal" and appropriate, if that is how you feel. You do not need to justify feelings to anyone, but if you want to find peace, then you need to understand them for yourself, and if you want support, then you do need to communicate with those you love.

Communication can be hard if you are still navigating the ins and outs of your emotions, but not harder than keeping it all inside.

It can be helpful to unleash. Not only for you, but for those around you to know that you are not in a great place and that may be all you care to share. Do not feel forced to give more than you are willing to. Take your time. Freak out if you need to. Apologize. Don't apologize if you feel that's right. Trust your gut, because in the words of the great Cara Alwill Leyba, "... that bitch knows what's up!"

As you begin to unravel with your emotions, you make begin to realize how powerful depression and grief can be. It can feel like a long, unending, crying and violent windstorm. However, as you begin dissecting why you are angry, what is your cause for pain and grief, what will make you happy and why will it make you happy, you may start to see that these are not static emotions. Meaning, what causes you anger, pain or grief right now, can be healed, but it can also show up in different ways as you grow and understand your feelings about infertility.

When asked how I approached my infertility depression, I don't answer it as if it's not happening anymore. I don't see the healing associated with infertility as a "one and done" scenario. It's not like you take it on and - *Ta-Da* – it's over.

Infertility is like a boo-boo that scabs over but never really goes away. At least it is for me. It is something that you can heal, but you don't ever really "get over" it. It's something that you build a muscle around, become stronger about, and decide if it will define you, or will you define it.

Simply put, over time things can get better, then go back to bad, and then onward to feeling better than ever, but back to moments of sadness and "why not me". Healing is not linear, so moments of back and forth will show up again, and again. Be patient with your process and take growth, healing, compassion, and dealing with feelings of pain, anger, and grief at your own pace. Remember, there is no right or wrong way to process your experience.

~

Along the path of communication, and while sharing your feelings with others, there will be responses to your grief that you just don't like. Straight up, it will piss you off and leave you wondering why you ever said anything in the first place? Don't be too hard on yourself when you find disappointment versus support. Also, don't be too hard on those who have zero clue how to comfort you or what it is that you need.

People are problem solvers remember? As humans, we often speak first; think second, and, while trying to be helpful, we say whatever comes to mind in an effort to avoid the dead-air conversations. Therefore, a large majority of the time the comments that come out of people's mouths are not about you, and that should make perfect sense. Especially, when it comes to topics with which we have no experience and those that are "uncomfortable" or sensitive in nature.

Think of the last time you talked to something you knew nothing about. I'd assert you had more questions than offerings of advice or you probably just said whatever came to mind. There's nothing wrong with it. It's just a matter of humanity and the fact that we do not live inside each other's bodies. We don't know the interworking of other humans. We live our own lives and have our own response, so when we speak on something it's generally from our own experience. And, if we have no experience, well, we can wind up saying a whole bunch of nothing or doing the best we can to offer support in our way.

I like to think we are all a bunch of confused "Bob the Builder's" walking around yelling, "Can we fix it?" and instead of screaming, "Yes we can!" the rest majority of us are looking around thinking, "I don't know? Maybe."

Point is what people think, say, or do is not about you, but if you are open to it, you can choose to see the intention is often good. You can choose to see that there are varying levels to friendship and relationships and not all of them can handle it when you need a shoulder to lean on. You can choose to see that how most people respond to anything has everything to do with them and nothing to do with you.

You could be looking for support and what you receive instead sounds like a judgment, criticism, or like they're blowing you off. Okay. I get that may be hard to take, but maybe that is their way of trying. Maybe, this is something they're uncomfortable talking about. Maybe, they're a "good time Sally" that only wants to be there for drinking on the weekends and not heartfelt conversations. Whatever it is, it's your responsibility to figure it out if you want something from them. Not theirs. And, while I hate to get all Tupac on you, not everyone is going to be able to handle heavy, heartfelt, and sensitive conversations. You can't blame them for it, but you can have awareness around it and accept, "that's just the way it is".

If you tell someone that you are struggling with infertility and they stutter or go "deer in a headlights' on you, consider their humanity. Consider, where you are in your processing, and they're still back at stage one in denial and shock. Cut them some slack, if you can, and give them some empathy, because you were once back there too. Even if they've known about your infertility struggle for some time, and they are not giving you what you need, there could still be an opportunity for some empathy or it could be time to give that relationship a heave-ho, but I'd urge you to consider empathy first.

Why? They're not forced to live with infertility and all that comes with it every day, so they're not as sensitive as you are from trying to survive, thrive, and heal. What anyone says to you as an offer of "advice" or "help" or "support" allow for it to be just that if you can.

See if you can receive their offer as encouragement and know it is more about them being there for you than it is about saying or doing the "right thing" because, let's be honest, there is no right thing. In fact, someone could say the "perfect" thing and there are moments where it could still piss you off depending upon the day of the week or "that" time of the month.

When sharing yourself focus on the strength it takes to do so and less on what it is you're hoping to get out of the other person as a measurement of their level of concern. Moments of vulnerability can be useful to you in the long run and help you see new access points to healing. Stay as open and receptive as sanely possible because it can go from helpful to emotional and back again real quick.

~

When people are uncomfortable, sometimes they say things just for sake of saying something. This is commonly known as verbal diarrhea. It is not meant to be harmful, but it is inevitable.

Here are a few examples of word vomit that I suggest you let roll down your back.
"You need to relax ...."
"When you have a baby, ..."
"God has a plan."
"When the time is right... ."
"It will happen when... ."

The people, who love you, love you, which is why they say anything at all. It would do your sanity good to remember that no matter how awkward, angry, or downright annoyed their comments may make you feel, their intention does not have to be malicious.

Their words can be a beacon of hope and faith, if you let it. They can be a reminder of your worth in a struggle that feels like it's sucking you down a deep dark hole and someone has just thrown you a lifeline reminder that you are not infertility. They can be an invitation to stop feeling like this is your fault and a way to tap into some peace. They can serve as a recognition that says, "Hey! This shit is tough, but so are you. Don't forget that!"

In the end, I'll own that there was a time or two where I found myself dangerously close to telling a co-worker, friend or family member to *kindly shut the fuck-up* for saying one or more of the aforementioned. I also may or may not have imagined an entire scenario where immediately following those comments, I mentally punched them in the face, and said, "Stop saying stupid shit you know nothing about!"

It is a lot of aggression. It is a lot of anger. It is a lot to hold on to on top of everything infertility already brings to your life. It's not wrong. It's not right. It happens and I completely own all of it.

I also own that it was exhausting. Walking around in fear that someone was going to ask me about infertility, say something I didn't like or offer some advice that was going to take me from Tinkerbell to Tyrannosaurus Rex. It sucked the life out of me.

As a result, I wasn't able to communicate with anyone about infertility because I was afraid. I was afraid of what they would say, think and how I might respond. This fear made it impossible for me to talk to others about how I was feeling. It also made it difficult to receive anything from anyone as a vote of confidence and support, but what I learned in the process was that I wasn't mad at them. I was just mad in general.

They didn't cause infertility. I didn't cause it. But, you better believe I was enraged about it. Thus, their comments, whether perceived as positive or not, could not have bettered or worsened the situation. Regardless, I didn't want to hear it.

I received their support and then judged it. I was judge and jury of everyone around me, freely casting verdicts of right or wrong. I wasn't doing it for fun. Trust, me when I tell you I wasn't having any fun. I was doing it to protect me. I was doing it to preserve the relationships. I was doing all of it because I was devastatingly hurt, and I couldn't bare the idea of possibly being hurt any more, so I invented a contraption that kept myself distanced from them and me closed off from feeling supported, heard, or loved. It was a vicious cycle and I was very committed to it.

The commitment to feeling justified in anger and isolation is a one-sided operation. I decided that no one could understand what I was going through. In service of that decision, I chose not to talk about it. In not talking, anything that anyone offered-up immediately became wrong and with that I got to be mad. It was a lose-lose situation, where I had convinced myself that I was in control and if I was in control then I couldn't get hurt. Right? Wrong. Again, I was just mad, so it became a toxic cycle of I'm mad, but now I get to be mad at more people than just me. Yay!

In this contraption of anger and trying to control everything, I discovered that I was doing it because it was an opportunity to be mad at something other than our struggle and someone other than me. However, it never made me feel any better. It never made the struggle go away. It only added aggression, rage, and conflict to a situation that already felt shitty, and to be honest, I didn't need to feel any shittier.

If you find yourself, developing an eye twitch to comments from anyone let alone those closest to you, I'd invite you to look at what's being said and your response to it. If it fires you up and you feel justified. Cool. I'm not going to tell you not to be in your feelings or allow yourself to be with whatever emotions show-up. However, I would urge you to consider seeing if you can find any encouragement in it. If you can, then stop resisting it and let it wash over you like a warm bath.

The love and support you receive, matched with the amount you are willing to give yourself, is what's going to pull you through this fucking thing. If you're triggered by a comment, then perhaps take the time to be with what about that comment is making you so angry. Maybe it's not the comment at all. Maybe it's not them. Dare I say it, Maybe It Is You? Maybe you are triggered because your emotions are on a level 1,000. Ok. While that may not be great to admit, at least you are giving yourself the opportunity to know.

Stop seeing who you are or how you feel as something that is wrong. What's going on, coupled with your strong emotions, may be undesirable, but you are human. How about you start allowing yourself to be one? What would like be like if you allowed yourself to know that you are flawed and messy? How would the relationship you have with others and yourself change if you permitted yourself to see everyone that way? What if you decided to allow those around you, who may not have any idea how you feel, the space to be human too? Can you choose to receive what is being offered to you, a comment, hug, or gift, as a gesture of support, before you decide to settle into mentally deeming them the village idiot and as someone who will never understand?

~

It is one thing to own whether or not we have become reactionary in our behavior. It is quite another to keep what hurts us inside.

Keeping shit in is toxic. I like to think of holding on to what hurts or perturbs us like vomiting. While I'd assert no one *likes* to throw-up, I've always been quite fond of the sentiment out with the bad and in with the good. If the body is telling you to get rid of something, let it out. Rid your body, life and energy of whatever it is, stop blocking yourself from doing it and air it out before it spoils like garbage.

Verbalizing how what someone has said or done made you feel is good for your soul and your relationship. If you give a shit about that person and the connection you have, holding on to feelings about it will only lead to bad things.

If you do not tell them, they will not know. This is not the psychic hotline. They are not predicting your feelings nor are they minimizing them. Perhaps, they were trying to be kind. Awesome! Perhaps, they were trying to offer support. Fantastic! Perhaps, they don't know what the fuck to say. Ok. Not the worst thing in the world. However, you won't know if you don't speak on it and if it's hurting or bothering you, it's up to you to decide if airing your grievances will better or worsen the situation.

The other side of it is, if you decide not to say anything, then you better be ready to own it. Do not carry resentment and hurt feelings around like a dead carcass. If you decide it's not worth speaking on, then that is on you. Do not project your anger or decisions on them.

Whatever happens, we're all human. That means it is very likely that at some point, we will say and do things that we don't mean. We do it in service of connection.

I'd like to believe it is not the goal of most people to hurt others. I'd like to believe that a large majority of the population is looking to give love and feel loved in return because it feels good. If someone says something that rubs you the wrong way, decide how valuable they are to your life and relationship. Decide if you believe their intention was to hurt you. Decide if it is something you need clarity around and if it is, it is up to you to speak on it.

At the end of the day, the people who are closest to you want to see you win. Consider anything they have to say as a vote of confidence. Decide if you can see that. Determine if you feel like they believe in you, love you, and value the contribution you bring to their life. If you don't, then it might be time to reprioritize the space they occupy in yours.

~

Depression is not something you just move past. If it was, there'd be a lot less people in the world feeling isolated in it, in therapy, or living in fear of judgment about it. It is not a one and done thing and it is not the same as sadness. With sadness, you meet the emotion and pass through it rather quickly, whereas with depression, the feelings of unhappiness, isolation, overwhelm, and lethargy, persist.

According to WebMd, depression can be described as a persistent combination of any of the following; daily sadness that continues throughout the day, trouble concentrating, remembering details, and making decisions, fatigue, feelings of guilt, worthlessness, and helplessness, pessimism and hopelessness, insomnia, early-morning wakefulness, or sleeping too much, irritability, restlessness, loss of interest in things once pleasurable, including sex, overeating or appetite loss, aches, pains, or headaches, persistent anxiousness, or "empty" feelings, and suicidal thoughts or attempts.

Some people live with depression their entire life, and others can experience depressive feelings. My infertility depression, while not clinically diagnosed, consumed me, took all my attention and energy, and was something I hid from everyone.

Of the aforementioned symptoms, I can see my depression and where I identify with it. I felt sadness that lasted all day everyday for what felt like 4 solid years, fatigue to the point where I barely left the house besides for work, guilt that I was ruining my husbands life, worthlessness in my femininity, helplessness because nothing was working to get me pregnant, pessimism that I could ever be happy again, taking 2-4 sleeping pills every night, erratic and unpredictable mood swings, zero sex drive, at 5'5 I found myself at 95 pounds, severe headaches and nervousness, and thoughts of suicide.

I felt so inundated with the amount of effort required to combat infertility that I couldn't allow myself to see that I was drowning in sorrow. Yet, I was painfully aware of it and equally ashamed at the same time. I was conscious of my feelings. I was terrified of them and in my mind, I was convinced that this is what I had to endure if I wanted a family, so I sucked it up and committed to get through it. I was so mad at myself for infertility that it became my cross to bear. It became my mountain to climb. It became my war to win and feeling sad 24/7, well, that just seemed logical.

While everyday felt like hell on earth, I had become the infertile equivalent of a Stepford Wife. Each day felt like I did the same thing on repeat. I woke-up at 5:30 AM, exercised, showered, applied my make-up while looking in the mirror and thinking how much I hated myself, did what I needed to do as far as fertility injections and taking prenatal vitamins, then it was off to the doctors to have my blood drawn, ultrasound done, or IUI executed, all before 8 AM.

After that, it was off to work where I'd survive the day like a Zombie, attend meetings, answer anyone who asked, "How are things going?" with a canned response, "Oh! Things are going great! Still plugging along. It will happen." then immediately following, I would cry in the bathroom for 5-10 minutes.

Before the day was over, I would return to autopilot, hit up a few more meetings, head home, cry in my car, curse God and the Universe, cook dinner for my husband, cry in the bathroom, and depending on the day, receive an HCG shot in my ass or push a progesterone pill into my vagina, take 2-4 sleeping pills and drift off into a drug induced state of restlessness where I dreamt about having children or the fear of never having one. My everyday was some version of this on repeat for what felt like an eternity.

Looking back I think *no wonder I was depressed,* infertility consumed my life. It became who I was and vice versa. I was obsessed with it. Having a child was the goal and utilizing fertility methods appeared to be the only way to achieve it, so the cycle of what I needed to do and the emotional rollercoaster that came along with it became necessary.

Infertility not only became a part of my life, but part of my identity. All accompanied it became normal, familiar, or a part of the deal. I guess you could say I saw it and the emotional distress as required.

Without a doubt, infertility made me feel bad, and the feelings of sadness and devastation that came with it it controlled my life. As a result, I couldn't feel genuine joy anymore. I didn't even know how to access it or if it was available to me. Melancholy became my natural state of being.

I was numb to happiness, humor, and love. They felt as if they were emotions that existed outside of me. They eluded me and while I wanted them, I didn't feel like I deserved them, because I wasn't happy.

Even though feeling this way scared the hell out of me and made me feel unrecognizable to myself, it also comforted me at the same time. I know that must sound weird. I was addicted to and comforted by persistent sadness, but it is true. I was so sad and devastated by infertility that it made sense to be depressed. It made sense because I viewed infertility as *my problem* and because it was mine, until I could get pregnant, I would be sad and had no business being happy. It was an endless cycle that had only one possible way out; get pregnant or be miserable forever.

The struggle of trying to have a baby became the *thing* to overcome. It became the pot of gold at the end of the rainbow. It was the journey I needed to see through to the end, while simultaneously, no longer wanting to be on. It was the thing that I wanted to stop letting define me. The carousel I desperately wanted to get off but couldn't. I saw no possible way to stop the cycle. Not until I was pregnant.

~

Pregnancy was the goal. It was the key to a happy life. It was the missing piece that would make me whole. If I could pregnant, then I could win. I could find love. I could find purpose. I could stop being *Shannon the girl who struggles with* infertility, and go back to being Shannon. I could stop the sadness, isolation, self-loathing, and guilt, and in its place find myself.

Everyday that went by, that I wasn't pregnant, was another day I fell deeper into my depression. Each day that I was depressed, it became more natural, less foreign, and like my life's destiny. The more I went on thinking this is the life I was meant to live and that joy was unavailable to me, the more I justified, related to, and found ease in wrapping myself in sadness. The more I allowed it to envelope me.

While I had found comfort in despondency, I could see, hear, and feel that I wasn't happy. I knew that what I wanted was to feel joy, find purpose, see myself as a strong, brilliant, sexy, beautiful human, and in all of that I would also feel peace again. I understood that at the moment I wasn't in that place, but being a Mother became the thing to aspire for. It became a trophy at the end of the infertility race. It ruled how I conditioned myself and how I lived my life. It dictated how I acted, lived, ate, exercised, slept, and had sex. It was my motivation for everything. It was the first thing I thought of every morning and the last thing at night.

Being a Mom became my reason for being and somewhere along the way became who I was even before I was one. It defined my life, accomplishments or lack thereof, and dictated the value of self worth. I had decided that in order to be happy Ever Again that I needed to win at infertility and to do that I needed to become a Mother.

Everything that I was became tied-up in our struggle with infertility. Shannon as a human being no longer mattered. My legacy and the sum of everything I was or could ever be became wrapped up in being a Mom.

If I couldn't be a Mom, then what was my purpose? Why was I even a woman? What value was I contributing to society if I couldn't procreate?

The answer, I decided, is that I was put on this planet to make babies and have children. If I couldn't do that, then I, Shannon, was of no value, and if I wanted to find value, then I needed to beat infertility. I needed to stay the course. I needed to win the race and if that meant depression was a side effect, well, that wasn't going to stop me, until it almost did.

Depression is not a joke but is also nothing to be ashamed of. As I shared before, the awareness I found around depression came when thoughts of suicide entered my mind. It was a shock to my system. It was the alarm that went off and finally triggered me to see that something deep was happening. Yes. I wanted to be a Mother. Yes. I wanted to have our baby. Yes. I was doing everything we could possibly do at the time to make it happen. No. It wasn't working.

When suicide entered the picture, I developed awareness about the depths of my infertility depression, but I still didn't see it as ruling my life. It was a pain in the ass. It was a constant struggle. It made me feel like shit and hate myself, but somehow, even with all of that, I wasn't able to see that it had become how I identified myself.

It became me. I became it. Even though I could feel the chokehold it had on my life, I didn't see that I was the one using it as a weapon.

You know that saying, "You can't see the forest through the trees." Yeah. It was a lot like that. I wanted a child, but I wasn't clear on how far I would go to get one. I wanted a family, and yet, it never occurred to me that I was already in one. I wanted to find purpose, and I had determined that it existed outside of me. I couldn't see that I was sacrificing myself for all of it. I knew what I was doing to my body, but I just didn't have space to see how the choices I was making were impacting everything else.

I was aware of the pressure, guilt, shame and blame, but I couldn't see how I was using all of it to push me forward. I wasn't relying on hope, faith and love to encourage me to continue to pursue fertility treatments. I could say that each month there was some of that sprinkled in there. However, in full transparency, I was using the fear of what it would mean if I didn't succeed to hold me accountable to the process, keep me consistent, and focus my mind on the goal. I guess you could say I was using "scare tactics" or "limiting beliefs" to beat me into submission, drown out the voices asking me who I had become, if this is the life I want to lead, and I used it to threaten myself to keep going.

I couldn't see the damage I was doing to myself. I couldn't see that I wasn't operating from a place of love, but fear. I couldn't see that I was lost, at least, not until a Saturday afternoon chat with my Mom.

~

I can't speak for everyone, but my Mom is the fucking best! She's empathetic and loving, yet, tough, powerful and crazy smart all at the same time. She is the only person I was semi-willing to talk to about infertility. I say semi because I didn't give her all the details, but everyone else got significantly less than her, so for me it was something.

One random Saturday afternoon while talking all things life with Mom, we got into a conversation about where we were in our infertility process. In almost every conversation, infertility was inevitably on the docket of discussion items. Every time the topic arose I found myself immediately annoyed. I didn't want to talk about it, because it felt like a never-ending horror story and yet, a part of me always felt a bit better when I did.

Talking about infertility was a constant tug-of-war. While I begrudgingly talked about it with my Mom, I always left the conversation feeling a little bit like someone gave a shit. It's true that I wasn't sharing much of my journey or feelings with anyone else, but nevertheless it meant something to me to feel heard.

This particular chat would be one that laid a brick in the road to healing on my journey of self-discovery with infertility. It gave me a sense of clarity. It allowed me to see what I needed in this struggle, who I had become in it, and how I wanted to move forward. It would be the first time I said out loud to anyone that I was tired. That everything involved with the treatments was taking a lot out of me, not to mention my bank account, and that the constant disappointment was becoming to tough to endure.

I felt guilty for admitting it. I felt weak for wanting to give up. I felt ashamed and scared that if I did stop the treatment process, then I would be ruining our chances of becoming a family. Yet, at the same time, I was terrified that if I didn't stop, then I would lose my mind.

In my head I knew it wasn't true. I knew infertility wasn't my fault, but I still couldn't explain away the hurt, anger, and guilt to my heart. I wanted so desperately to have a family and yet, I wanted to quit doing all of it? What the fuck? Who does that?

I didn't understand it. I didn't understand anything or myself anymore. All I knew was that I felt like I was losing myself, and it scared me shitless. I wanted to stop being scared. I wanted to stop feeling worthless. I wanted to go back to the way life was before infertility, but I knew I couldn't. I knew I couldn't change what had happened, but I needed release!

I needed to find a way to make infertility stop meaning something was wrong, broken, or defective about me. I wanted to stop making it the *thing* that defined me. I wanted to stop hating God, the Universe, and myself for it, but the pain surrounding all of the disappointment, time, money, and energy spent was so great that I didn't know how. I had surrendered to a life that I wanted as a Mother. I didn't know how to surrender to what it would mean about it me if –after all of this- I couldn't be one.

I shared all of it with Mom through inconsolable sobbing. Unloading each layer of uncensored truth, she listened and waited. She watched and observed. She let me get it all out. I blacked out. I unleashed. Mere minutes felt like hours and by the end of it, I was all but screaming, hyperventilating, and dizzy.

"Breathe", she said. I did. It was about all I could do.

For an instant, I felt like I had just taken a 500 lb weight off of my back for the first time in years. I felt lighter. I felt release. Feeling afraid and exposed, of course, immediately followed this outburst.

It didn't matter if this was my Mom. It didn't matter that I know she loves me and has cared for me her whole life. It didn't matter if it was Jesus Christ, himself. Mind you, if it had been, I assure you I would have definitively asked him, "WHAT THE FUCK DUDE? WHY ME?" None of that mattered. Infertility made me judge myself enough and sharing my true feelings about it made me feel available for judgment.

I remember thinking, "Please don't say anything to piss me off. PLEASE!" I didn't know what would piss me off and in those days anything would. I remember feel my defenses immediately go up. We were on thin ice and even though I didn't tell her, something in her being said she knew.

Uttering not a single word, I studied her face as she studied mine. I observed her mannerisms as I unraveled and fell a part. I pretended to gain composure and gave her a half-witted smile to put her at ease, but mostly, it was me putting up a shield of defense. I don't know why I felt the need to protect her, but I did. I had exposed her to the mess that is her daughter and guilt and worry flooded my mind. I didn't want to be a burden to her, and I didn't want her to think that I had gone insane.

I watched her confusion turn to reservation, fear to rescue, and her support to curiosity. As she watched me breakdown, lose my breath, and melt into a puddle of emotions before her, she returned a look that I think only Mom's can give. She looked at me with eyes that said *I wish I could take this all away* and *I would take this on for you if I could* and with that look, she said, "So, take a break."

I was mad at her for saying it and I loved her for it at the same time. I was angry because I wanted her to give me some pep talk about "keep going". Yet, I admired her for seeing that I was suffering and saying the thing I believe she knew would be tough for me to hear anyway.

She felt my hardship. She heard me. She saw that I was exhausted and I couldn't stay in the fight any longer. She got that I needed permission to grant myself release.

My emotions were somewhere in-between wanting to jump through FaceTime and scream *you don't know how this feels,* and hugging her. I had never felt so scared and alone, but also loved and understood in all of my life.

238

I sat and let her words sink in. I took a breath and then said, "I can't." She immediately and rapidly asked, "Why?" I took another deep breath and angrily became filled with thoughts of regret, resentment, and self-judgment. I took a breath and I cried harder still.

She waited, again. She let me have space to lose my shit, again, and I finally said, "Who am I if I can't have a child?"

She said, "What do you mean?"
I said, "What is my legacy if I can't produce a family?"

Again, she sat and looked at me, but this time her brow furrowed, her eyes looked intense. She stopped and gave me the Mom look. You know the one that makes you think something intensely scary or awesome is about to happen, and with all her infinite Motherly wisdom and all the grace of a woman who has lived, she said the best thing I have ever heard and still hold onto to this day.

She said, "Your legacy isn't other people. Your legacy began the minute you were born and will continue on long after you are dead. Your legacy is you."

If that shit doesn't just blow your mind, then I don't know what will. It was so wise. It was so on point. It had never occurred to me that by simply existing I am creating my legacy every day in all that I do and do not do. It shot a jolt direct from my brain down into my heart and soul and it hit me deep and hard. It made me pause and I cried again, harder still.

I'd be lying if I said that there wasn't some part of me that felt like my Mom was placating me that day. That she was trying to reach-out to her child, who was so obviously lost, and get through to her. That she was looking for a way to offer me self-soothing. That she was a bit terrified about where I was and wanted me to step back from the cliff that I was on, instead of jump off it. I get all of that. However, what she said really struck a chord with me.

I am my own legacy. It made sense to me. Maybe it made sense because my Mother so obviously knows her child. Maybe it made sense to me because long before *Infertility Shannon,* or *Shannon as a Mom,* I was just Shannon. I didn't want to be married. I didn't want to have kids. I just wanted to be and know myself. I didn't define myself as those things. I was just me.

> Yes. I grew and learned about love and life, met a man whom I love, and I agreed to be married.
> Yes. I grew some more, learned about family and marriage, and we decided to have a kid.
> Yes. The second part wasn't going as planned and it felt like my whole life had turned to shit.
> Yes. Infertility made me feel like my life would only ever be ½ as good as it could be.
> Yes. I grew and learned about infertility.
> Yes. I did all that so I could to have a baby and here I am without one.

No. It doesn't mean I'm a quitter because I chose to stop treatments.

No. It wasn't love or empowered thinking that made me feel like infertility is my fault.

No. My life doesn't have to be ½ as good.

No. It doesn't mean a family isn't available to me.

No. I'm not weak, powerless, worthless, unlovable, or broken.

No. Infertility isn't my fault.

No. My friend, it isn't YOURS either.

Maybe me as my own legacy made sense, because it reminded me that at one point I knew myself, loved myself, and felt empowered to grow and learn from that self-love, but in the darkness of our struggle I didn't know how to access that anymore. Maybe it was what I needed to hear and at a time in which I was ready to hear it. Maybe I was done and I just needed someone to tell me it was OK. I don't know why that conversation with my Mom, on that day, illuminated how I was living and how deep of a depression I was in, but whatever it was, it was a stepping stone laid that would begin the process of me bringing myself back to life.

I had lost my way. I had stopped connecting to myself as the source of my joy. I couldn't find the value in life. I couldn't see the value in myself. There's something synchronistic and serendipitous about the fact that this realization occurred following a conversation with the person who gave me life. Something beautiful in having someone who loves you reflect to you all the ways in which you are not loving yourself.

I had made infertility the focus of my life. The idea to have a family was born from love, but I had decided that the joy within it was contingent upon whether or not I could have a baby. I had stopped growing and learning who I was in our struggle the minute I decided that if I couldn't produce a child, then I would not be worthy of love. The minute I decided that, was the exact moment I stopped loving myself

~

Once you've realized that infertility has taken a Kung Fu grip on your life and not even ninja like maneuvers can help you, you've basically hit second base and are rounding in on third. This is not time to pack-up your bags and go home. This is the time to stand and defend your life.

Do you want to be sad forever? Or, do you want to find a way to understand your feelings, your grief, take the time you need to be sad, and process all of it so you can still find a way to have a giggle? If the answer is yes, then do not give up now. You're steps away from realizing that you are not stuck but you are feeling your way through a difficult time and that is completely natural and appropriate.

There is nothing more alienating than wanting to feel happy but being unable to truly it. When you've mired in feelings of depression for too long you develop a sensation that you are unable to truly feel joy and that sucks because it is not for a lack of trying. Being brutally honest with yourself is the only way you will get to the other side of this.

Questions to ask yourself about your depression/grief.
Am I sad?
What is making me sad?
Am I talking to anyone about my feelings?
Why am I not talking to anyone about my feelings?
Is it helping me to not talk about my feelings?
What am I doing to help me understand my feelings?
Do I often sit alone in a dark room?
Do I often have outbursts of crying?
Do I self medicate?
Do I use things (i.e. food, alcohol, exercise, etc.) to avoid thinking/feeling?

You have all the answers you will ever need but sometimes you need help. I encourage you, have encouraged you, and will continue to encourage you to focus on your self-worth first. If your destiny is to be a parent, other options will present themselves but what matters now is having a solid foundation of value within yourself.

I believe people are magic. I believe we are capable of taking any life circumstance and bending it to our will with a little bit of work, okay, sometimes a fuck ton of work, but also a little faith. I believe with work we can create any life we want.

I do not believe that because things don't go our way that we should give up on the fairytale or that somehow a fairytale life eludes us. That's bullshit. Believing that you can't have the fairytale does not make people feel bad for you. It suggests tough love. That you feel bad for yourself and being entitled to have things go your way.

It is true. Some people have very plush lives and a lot of things go their way. If you are reading this, it is very likely that you are not one of those people. I apologize in advance for your hardship but I wrote this so you're kinda my people and I'm happy to know you.

Depression and grief are very serious. In your struggle with infertility, both can make you feel like you are unworthy of your fairytale because it didn't come easy.

The fact is plenty of people deal with hardship in their life. This is not to minimize the hardship you are in or your feelings about it, but you cannot willingly stay where you are, without helping yourself or seeking help, and expect people to feel bad for you. If you're reading this, and think you might be in an infertility depression or grieving, you owe it to yourself to figure this out. You are responsible for your life and, therefore, you are responsible for how you live it. Your choice.

CHAPTER 11:
LOVE IS THE ANSWER.

W hile never becoming a parent may have initially seemed like the most egregious part of your infertility diagnosis, I hope that after reading stages one through four you are starting to see things a little different. I hope you see the scariest thing about infertility is not that you can't have a baby. I expect me saying as such to still give you a moment of pause but I hope you find truth in acknowledging that infertility is not life altering because you cannot have one. Infertility is life altering because you want a child and the emotional aftershocks of realizing that may never happen is what sets you off-kilter.

The scariest thing about infertility shouldn't be reduced to having or not having a baby. I'm sure there are people out there who disagree with me and for whom this makes quite angry. Everyone is entitled to an opinion. Hell, I wrote an entire book on opinions. By the way, thanks for reading. Love ya, mean it! However, if you are someone who believes the life-altering aspects of infertility are summed-up in that you cannot have a baby, then you need some help in the "self-love" department.

Tough Love: Infertility is a fucked-up scenario front to back, the whole kit and caboodle, and not the cute kind where you can store your jewelry and such. It is not just about having a baby; it is that plus the emotional shit storm it brings to your life when it kicks your ass like it had been waiting for you at the bike rack for 25 years. Infertility will fuck your shit-up whether you currently value yourself or not. It

Infertility is not singularly about the fact that you cannot naturally have a baby, no matter how much it feels like that right now. It is about how the diagnosis affects you. It is about how negatively it makes you feel about your life and everyone in it. It is about how aggressively shock, anger, and grief culminate into one strong emotional depression and how that depression influences the negative way you treat yourself and others. It is about all the energy you put into feeling sad, angry, or depressed. It is about the unpredictability that surrounds it and now your life. It is because at best infertility reinforces the idea that life at its core is uncertain and you didn't think having a family was going to be one of the innumerable uncertainties in life.

Infertility is more than the sum of its parts. It is a movement and that movement, if you let it, it will depress your life and control how you feel about everything in or around it. Infertility isn't just about a baby. It is an emotion. It's a loss, grief, mystery, loneliness, abandonment, alienation, uncertainty, and identity. Infertility is about risking your happiness on uncertainty, taking this disease head-on, and going through how easily it makes you diminish your self-worth into two buckets.

Two buckets:

> Bucket number one says, "I have value if I can get pregnant." Hmmm... that sounds an awful lot like bargaining. In this bucket lives sunshine and roses.

> Consequently, the other bucket says, "I have no value, because I can't get pregnant." Ooh, I'd know that smell of depression anywhere. This bucket gives you rejection, alienation, anger, shock, grief, and pain.

As the barrier between getting what we want and happiness feels increasingly impossible, we turn inward and convince ourselves that we are part of the problem. From there, blame and rejection take precedent over nurturing and, because it is impossible to get away from you, you embark on an endless journey into self-loathing.

Through bargaining and depression, you learn that while trying to attain a fairytale you forgot to love you. As a result, you're sacrificing love for an ideal life and when it became unattainable your focus shifted to blame. In the name of a life that was never yours, infertility not only forces you to recognize your limitations but also your own mortality. It forces you to take hold of your fairytale, stand it next to your life, evaluate the comparisons, and ask yourself: if you can't have a baby, will the life you are currently living ever be enough?

The fact is infertility is real. It is also individual. There are alternative solutions for achieving parenthood status and we will get to that later but for now, it's important that you consider facts.

Other people may have a fairytale to you because they can get pregnant simply by having sex. I affectionately call them "breeders". So what? "The breeders" of the world having kids at a whim doesn't change your scenario. You need to accept that.

You are no less deserving of a fairytale life because you can't get pregnant the "old fashioned way". God, I hate that saying. It's so fucking dumb. There's nothing old fashioned about sex. You either have it or you don't. It's not a rickety old fence. It's sex and when you have it you don't get pregnant. You need to accept that.

Nothing will change the fact that your situation is afflicted by infertility, whether it is you or your partner that struggles, it all fucking sucks. I'm with you. Fist pound. You need to find a way to make it less "that fucking sucks" and more this is my reality because it is your reality. You need to accept that.

You are not defined by your infertility. Unless your name is literally, Infertility Smith, stop identifying yourself as someone who is summed-up to anatomy. You can't have a baby when you have sex; stop making that your entire life. If your life feels unfulfilled, it's because you're choosing to see it that way. You need to accept that.

You can still have a fairytale life but you need to figure out what that looks like. This will require time, patience, honesty, love, and work. See notes one to four above and take them into consideration. You need to accept it... all of it.

~

I'd like to say that the carryover from bargaining and depression to depression and acceptance is an easier one but unfortunately, none of this is easy. Except, there is one very important thing will occur in stage five; healing. Happy Dance!

The idea of healing may make you feel like crying happy tears. After all you've been through, stage five is your victory lap in understanding your life and what you will continue experience until you accept this is happening.

Bargaining and depression help us identify behaviors that keep us in the past and, by allowing us to see it, it makes perfect sense to mourn the loss of our fairytale. Depression and acceptance will help us understand we weren't wrong for manifesting a "perfect life" and wanting it.

Depression and acceptance help us to see that wanting what we want makes us human. It is natural to want a life that makes you happy and to feel disappointment over the loss of it. Depression and acceptance will help you to see there is no such thing as perfect and there never was. Rather, there is a different reality available to everyone and in your reality you will need to choose to adapt for the sake of being happy.

In an effort to say this as clearly as possible, in stage four, we discuss your ideal life and how so much of your adult happiness is hinged on circumstances within it. The life you desire is a fairytale. It is an idea. It's not wrong. It just is. Clearly, it is a common idea that many people share and often achieve. However, it was never a guarantee. The mantra is often heard, "To have a family, is to have been blessed." We can acknowledge this as true because even if you are estranged from your family you have one and they gave you life. At minimum, I don't think it is too much to suggest that you can throw-out a, "Thank you! Hell-yes for life!" However, if you cannot have a family, does that make you any less blessed? Does it make your life or the people in it any less of a blessing?

I hope your answer is No, as in you wouldn't reject all the goodness and blessings you already have as sacrifice for a baby. Your life is whatever you make it. If you want it to be amazing, get up and do something about it. No one is going to make you take the initiative to engage in your reality and see how many opportunities you have this very moment.

Infertility sucks! Again, I will confirm your feelings on this. No one likes to feel they're in the "reject" pile. No one wants to feel unworthy of parenthood. I get it. Allow yourself to own your feelings on this. Indulge your grief because it is worthy of feeling however you need to feel about it, and accept that either you want to live a fulfilling life or you don't.

Having a family is an idea we strive to achieve because it is what we're programmed to believe is our greater purpose on this big round ball of gas, gravel, and liquid. It makes sense to place such a high regard on procreating, parenting, and assigning value to our lives based on having parental relationships and children as our greatest contribution to the world.

> It makes complete sense that the idea of never having a family comes as a shock to you.
> It makes complete sense that you define your legacy by the humans you leave behind.
> It makes complete sense the idea of never having children makes you angry, sad, and depressed.
> It makes complete sense that you would be willing to sacrifice almost anything to feel normal and reverse this diagnosis if you could.

Do you know why all of this makes total sense? Because it never occurred to you that it wouldn't be possible for you until infertility.

All of the emotions in all stages call us to take great responsibility for things in our lives that others may never have to deal with. I can think of at least five people right now, some in my own family, who never take responsibility for their actions, who never take accountability for their life let alone how it affects others, and who do not think about their contribution to the world and what that even means.

Do not pat yourself on the back because you pause to understand how your actions are not only affecting you but all those around you. Don't you dare, Miss Congeniality! That shit is what's wrong with the world today. We're self-absorbed and have our heads so far up our own asses that we never bother to think about what someone else is going through. We never pause and contemplate the possibility someone else is in a difficult time and maybe they don't want to hear about how your dog sniffs other dogs' asses everywhere you go. No one cares, Barb! Point is you're not given some right of passage to pat yourself on the back because you take time to process how infertility has temporarily fucked all kinds of shit up in your life. Nope. This is not going to be like your nephew's t-ball game where everyone gets a trophy. This is accountability. This is responsibility. This is you taking the time to own your shit, seize your life, and feel genuinely happy in it. The reward is in the effort. So, no, there will not be a trophy at the end of this. However, there will be you living in a life that you are inspired by.

Depression can make you feel weighed down by your feelings, but it also allows you to see a responsibility to understand them. Think about it, you didn't start your life with a husband and two kids. Years of fairytales and chick flicks helped you to develop this idea.

You developed an image of the perfect life in your head overtime. Your life actually started as just you. Yes. You had a mom, dad, and potentially, brothers, Jim-Bob and Jordan, but you didn't start out with a life assignment: get married and have kids or die trying.

As humans, we are ambitious in our fairytale personas. We often view ourselves as superhuman or supermodel. I, myself, often wake-up hoping I'll look just like Halle Berry. It hasn't happened yet but my persistent disappointment doesn't seem strong enough to make me stop hoping. In matters that are trivial, like being a replica of Halle Berry, the emotion and the drive do not support each other like they do within the hope and disappointment of infertility.

Our ambitions aren't driven by what is achievable or not. If that were the case, America wouldn't have so many entrepreneurs and I wouldn't want to look like Halle Berry. Our ambitions are driven by what we want not by what we believe is actually attainable. In light of this, it's completely understandable that it never occurred to you, you would need to find a way to cope in the event you couldn't have your perfect life. This is where disappointment and depression take hold of you and cause you to identify yourself as being unable to achieve happiness.

It is not that you cannot be happy. Rather, it's that you need to process your feelings and adjust your thinking. It is more than acceptable for you to grieve the loss of your fairytale but it is important that you don't miss your life in the process. Once you decide that you want to be happy and that living a life is far greater than not living at all, you have decided to take-on the weight of acceptance.

Right about now, you might feel pretty beat-up. You might feel like you have taken just about as much as anyone can take before breaking and, right before you do, a light turns-on in the back corner of your mind. It's candlelight so it's not bright but it is enough to create a flicker and illuminate a small space. In this area, sits your happiness. It's been patiently waiting for you to remember it.

You became so consumed with feelings of fear, resentment, avoidance, and grief that locked your happiness away. Don't beat yourself over the head with this. You didn't know you locked your happiness away. It came on unknowingly the minute someone told you that your Happily Ever-After wasn't going to play-out exactly like you thought. I'm no PhD. but I believe this is called self-preservation.

In response to your shock, anger, depression, all of it, you guarded your feelings of happiness away in hopes that someday you would be able to come back to them and I'm happy to tell you that you can. When the green light to happiness reveals itself that means some serious emotional, mental and physical processing has gone down. It means that you are ready to take acknowledge and embrace that they still exist for you.

When you decide you are ready to get your happy-on, don't expect to be the same person you were before you entered this emotional journey. You've been to hell and back, it is unrealistic for you to go toe to toe with some seriously emotional shit and come out the other side unscathed. When you encounter a life-altering situation like infertility, it changes you.

~

In a conversation with my husband discussing how I felt at my lowest, I explained to him the rage I felt towards God for withholding a child from our life for so long and after every effort we made. I listed off time after time that I declared to religion that I did not need it anymore because in my time of need I felt like it had forsaken me.

Not only were we childless and I was a religious reject, but I had become an outsider to myself. I lost my femininity, confidence, and ability to nurture me.

Would I call myself a religious person today? No. I wouldn't but I wouldn't say I am not religious either. I would say that this experience has driven me to become more spiritually aligned. It has afforded me the opportunity to have as much faith in the known as the unknown. It has allowed me to believe in my energy and that of the world around me. It has allowed me to see that what I emote out it what I will receive back. It has allowed me to see that I have the opportunity to decide how my life is going to go versus the relationship I had previously in which I relied upon God, prayer, or a bible to dictate my behaviors.

I am not judging religion. I am judging the relationship I had to it. It was one in which I thought there was something in this world better equipped to make decisions for me. It was me putting all the power outside of myself. It was me believing I was ill-equipped to have power and make good choices with it. It was me thinking that I needed to rely on what existed outside of me more than what was within me.

The knowing that I developed through infertility was not the denouncing of religion. I believe in a higher power. Some people call it God, Buddha, Jehovah, or Source Energy. I just see it as a force or energy, one that we all have access to harness, embody and put out into the world. I see it as being gift that we all have the ability to access and share, but it is dependent upon deciding to see it as available to us.

The knowing that came with seeing my pattern of wanting to rely on something outside of me as being the reason for my growth, strength, and being was in the acceptance of self. It was in knowing that no matter what happened, no matter if I was wildly successful or a major failure, I could always thrive as long as I believed in me. I didn't have to always put my faith in something else. I could begin to see the beauty, capacity for greatness, and abundance of life by starting to believe in me more than anything else.

The knowing that came with loving, growing into, and appreciating myself was a liberated kind. It liberated me to understand that I truly know nothing. Typing this actually makes me laugh, because it's so true.

We as humans look at what we do know and catalogue it as a form of validation. I validate my being by seeing myself as a constant evolution. Therefore, I cannot possibly know everything. I cannot tell you what is going to happen an hour from now let along 1 year from today. It's freeing to find that kind of clarity. One that suggests, I know what I know in the moment but in 2.5 milliseconds from now that can grow and significantly change and with it so can I. While I don't have certainty about what cards I will be dealt, or who I am going to become as a result, I can be committed to whom I am going to be about it.

I can be committed to showing up from my heart. I can be committed to learn and grow. I can be committed to understanding that nothing is certain and with that uncertainty welcome change. The knowing that came with my commitment to who I wanted to be freed me from trying to make sense of life. It freed me from looking at what does or doesn't materialize as "good" or "bad". It allowed me to see that there is good in the bad and bad in the good and I can decide that I want to be in love with that. I can decide that this life is uncertain at best and the sooner I respected that fact, the less angry I became.

In that same conversation, my husband asked me what I thought the difference was between heaven and hell? It gave me pause and made me think about my depression and the thoughts I had about life during that dark time. What came up is I don't know if there is a heaven and I don't know if there is a hell. I imagine that if there is a hell the people in it live in a state close to what I lived in during my dark time.

257

They are filled with rage, hate, envy, and fury. They are constantly questioning their surroundings with an insatiable appetite for understanding and looking for answers in everything else but themselves. Their quest for validation and sadness runs so deep that the longing for happiness has left them and in its place they choose to continue questioning what they will never find answers to.

Why would one do this? I don't think it is an exact science, but from my experience, I would assess that it is to punish ourselves and in doing this we can never find acceptance because the power forever lives outside of us. It exists in believing that there must be a reason for everything. It is exists in believing that there is only good and bad. It exists in believing that bad thins only happen to bad people, but that's not true. Bad things sometimes happen to good people and there is no answer for why. Sometimes the only answer is that it just does.

Jean Paul Sartre said, "Hell is other people." Taken literally, you might think this means that we as people cannot stand other humans. However, it actually is a reference to the fact that we cannot stand the perception of ourselves. We develop an awareness of who we think we are or who we need to be and then as a result detest that which we have become. Therefore, hell is not other people, it is the essence of what we do not like about who we have become.

Coming out on the other side of a struggle, your whole life may look different. You may feel different. You may act different. Hopefully, you find freedom; excitement and value in knowing that in the face of the hardships you face you get to be new. This isn't something you need to feel ashamed of but I do recommend that you allow yourself to be aware of and compassionate about it.

~

If going through "something" makes you feel inadequate, don't beat yourself down. Tell people, give them the credit to hear you and relate to you, and quite possibly understand you. If you're going through something and you don't tell anyone, if they're the people closest to you, they're still going to understand. Be prepared to come out on the other side a little tattered and worn-out. Physical signs of emotional distress can cause weight loss, weight gain, hair loss, sleep deprivation, and signs of premature aging. Don't expect to think, feel, and look exactly the same. Don't expect to be the same. Period.

I don't want to tell you infertility will affect your physical appearance because it may not. Everyone's journey is different so everyone's chemical response can be different too. That being said, I don't want to tell you infertility won't affect your physical appearance because it can be alarming if it does. I know.

It may seem evident that when you take fertility drugs or try surgery to assist with infertility, there could be visual side effects. It wasn't to me.

Prior to fertility drugs, I never took anything other than Tylenol or Advil. This was in my chart. However, no one said I could lose weight, experience hair loss or growth, skin cysts and discoloration, or hypersensitivity to the sun. It was not pretty.

Additionally, I never had surgery prior to choosing it as an option to diagnose endometriosis so I was not aware how long it would take to heal from laparoscopy. They said 5 days. I can tell you it took me longer than 5 days.

While I don't want to scare you, I cannot in good conscience gloss over the physical damage that can occur if you pursue surgery or use infertility drugs to try and become pregnant.

~

A part of accepting infertility is accepting there are a finite number of options available to make you a parent. This book isn't about getting pregnant. It is an autobiography meets self-help hybrid that will hopefully help you process your feelings about infertility. The goal is to help you distinguish how you are or are not dealing with your what is happening to you and in identifying it, help you get reacquainted to your value.

That said, let me just repeat myself for clarity's sake, this is not a guide to help infertile people get pregnant. I am not going to tell you the ways you can go about getting pregnant but I will share with you our experience from the options we have tried.

Penis and Vaginas. Penis's go into vagina's and that is how babies are made. I don't know why anatomy decides we need to have sex to have a baby. It's weird and when I think about it, it seems aggressive. Not to mention, when I learned that the female body receives sex as a trauma to the vagina... well, some things you can't unlearn. Either way, I will tell you that the number of times my husband and I didn't use a condom, both before and after marriage, significantly outweighs the number of times we did. The point is to conceive "naturally" having sex is the only way to do it.

My husband and I were together for 5 years before we got married, and 6 months after that, is when I knew something had to be wrong. Consider that's 5 years of unprotected sex and no baby. If you discover that it's been more than a year, and you're still sans baby, then you may want to consider seeking a fertility specialist. If you discover that you are facing infertility, there are so many things to consider about your relationship before you jump into alternatives. After all, "Baby Band-Aids" do not fix marriages or relationships. Similarly, having a baby does not make a Man or a Woman a parent. Therefore, infertility is an opportunity to check-in on your relationship and get clear on how each of you defines family, what it is you can or cannot be with about this diagnosis, and if you're in agreement about next steps.

Doctors and Knives. I went to a fertility doctor when we weren't pregnant after having unprotected sex for several months. After nonchalantly explaining a diagnosis for Irritable Bowel dysfunction, frequent urination, extremely painful periods, and unprotected sex, a few tests later it was determined that my symptoms suggested I had endometriosis.

After further review of my symptoms, surgery was suggested to get us pregnant. Following surgery, we discovered the endometriosis was suffocating my left fallopian tube and ovary, and attached itself to my vagina and rectum. In addition, a sizable tumor was found inside my uterus. They labeled it an aggressive form of endometriosis: stage IV. For some, having the endometriosis removed does produce successful results for reducing painful periods and cramping, as well as increases conception.

I suggest seeing a fertility doctor if any of the above symptoms sound like you. I'm not telling you to pursue surgery. I chose this option because it appeared as if it was a problem solution scenario. Problem – Solution: If I get the endometriosis removed from my body and we have sex, we get a baby! It didn't turn out that way for us but that doesn't mean it won't for you.

Doctors, Penises, and Vaginas. After surgery, we did what is called a post-coital. You get a cocktail of steroids and hormones and you go to the doctors' like every freaking day to have them take blood, check your cervix, and do ultrasounds to review the maturity of your eggs and count. As you near ovulation, which is when your ovaries are ready to release an egg, the doctors tell you to have sex. You have sex for several days until your ovulation cycle ends and then you wait.

When you're 22 with raging hormones, having sex everyday for 3-5 days sounds really hot but when you're 29, work full-time, and are paying for this to work but each month it does not, trying to get pregnant becomes a job. The best piece of advice I can offer here is to get real comfortable with visiting your local sex store or find some porn that stimulates you both because sex can become less F.U.N. and more like W.O.R.K.

A few days post-coital, which means after sex, the doctor calls you back for a blood test to measure your HCG hormone. The HCG hormone, human chorionic gonadotropin, is produced during pregnancy. If the hormone is present in your body, then you're pregnant. It didn't turn out that way for us but that doesn't mean it won't for you.

Doctors and Basters. When Doctors, Penises, and Vagina's aren't getting the job done; it's time to up the ante... with everything. I'm talking more drugs to get more eggs, more doctors' visits to monitor your hormones, to more ultra sounds to check the size of your eggs, and let's not forget more money. From being told us to reserve our sperm and sex for ovulation, we graduated from having the doctor's tell us when to have sex, to give us your sperm and we'll put it in there.

Yup! No sex required. This sexiness is called an IUI. The official name is intrauterine insemination. This occurs when you're ovulating. In an IUI scenario, the doctor will take a tube that looks like a turkey baster, load it up with some sperm, and place the swimmers into the uterus.

The turkey baster is a thin flexible catheter-like tube that is passed into the vagina, through the cervix, and into the uterus. Typically, this will occur once the doctor has determined you have a mature egg.

What? Okay, let me break this down into the simplest way I can put this. You're on all these drugs to control your hormones and make sure you can produce a mature egg. A mature egg is one that is primed and ready to be penetrated by a sperm. When you do have a plump egg, then you get a shot of FSH in your butt, trusting someone capable of "shooting-up" your ass is mucho important here, and you administer this at home.

FSH is a follicle-stimulating hormone that sends a message to your ovaries that it is now time to release the eggs. Within 24 hours of getting shot in the ass, you go and get your turkey basted.

The doctor takes the sperm and shoots them right into your uterus. After a few days, the doctor calls you back for a blood test to measure your HCG hormones present during pregnancy. If the hormone is present in your body, then you are pregnant. It didn't turn out that way for us but that doesn't mean it won't for you.

The IUI process is pretty much the same for IVF - in-vitro fertilization – except you don't rely on the sperm to swim their way to the mature egg. With IVF, the fertilization of the egg occurs outside of the body and is then placed inside the vagina. My husband and I did not pursue this option for 2 reasons:

1. It is expensive.

2. After years of struggling to heal from depression, surgery, post coital's, and doctors with turkey basters, we decided to pause. We're currently still on pause with no plans to pursue IVF but that doesn't mean it won't be great for you.

Papers and Babies. This is also commonly known as adoption. Adoption is a popular and appropriate solution for those who struggle with infertility, have processed their emotions about the fact that they may never carry a child on their own, have embraced acceptance, and still want to be parents.

Similar to IVF, adoption is expensive and for reasons stated about IVF, after years of struggling to heal from a breakdown, financial and physical exhaustion, we decided that chilling seems to be working best for us. We currently have no plans to pursue adoption but that doesn't mean we can't change our mind and it doesn't mean it won't be a satisfying option for you.

Magic Needles. The next method is probably one of the most controversial methods but it has been my favorite. It's because it has helped me heal in many ways. The magic needles I refer to are acupuncture.

Acupuncture is the practice of using needles penetrating the skin to stimulate certain points on the body, to alleviate pain, increase circulation, or help treat health conditions.

Tiring of my depression, the injections, probing, and fertility drugs, we decided it was time to stop using a Western Medicine approach. I wanted my hair to grow back, my skin to stop breaking out with painful cysts, and to start feeling like I was connected to my body. Again, this is my interpretation of how the Western approach to infertility made me feel. I am not suggesting it is how you will feel: so don't allow your "take-away" to be that everything prior to Magic Needles sucks! No. It just sucked for us, that's all. Any who, finding acupuncture changed my life.

We did the top to bottom acupuncture approach which includes taking a daily vitamin and natural herbs, changing our diet to eat clean and whole foods more often than not, as well as adding calm life practices such as Yoga, and having sex when we wanted to, for love, and for fun! That's it!

There were no weekly ultrasounds. No chemicals. No looking like secretly I harbored an addiction because I've had my blood drawn from the same two arms everyday for 16 months. Acupuncture was less stressful, not to mention less invasive, it drastically reduced my cramping, and clotting. I love everything about it and I still do.

Was acupuncture anymore successful in getting us pregnant than the Western medicine? No. It didn't work out that way for us but that doesn't mean it won't for you.

We are currently not pregnant and no acupuncture did not work for us but I continue to do it because it has helped bring calm to my life, my mind, and changed the way I see myself, improved my sleep, decreased the amount of pain and for how long I am in it during a period, decreased the amount of clotting I have with a period, and has changed the amount of anxiety or anxious reactions I have in life. Sometimes, things don't have to work out the "right way" to still work.

~

In terms of finding acceptance, you must remain cautious because life is a slippery slope. Meaning, it is easy to feel like you're on an upswing or in the midst of a downward spiral when suddenly life swoops in and catches you off-guard. That is the glory of life. It has unexpected highs and lows. Just when you think it can't get any better, boom: the government sends you a check for $100. That is $100 you didn't have before; take it as a win! Then, just when you think life can't get any worse, boom: your cat dies. That cat helped you survive many poor decisions, moves, and subpar relationships; it only makes sense that you'd be heartbroken. It's just the nature of things. There will be great moments, shitty ones, time where you think life couldn't get any better and those where it's so bad you feel like you might just die.

As I mentioned, you will encounter many life-altering things along your life journey, with or without infertility, and there is no limit to the number that will challenge you. When processing transformative moments, it is important we don't forget to allow ourselves a moment of pause to grasp how we're feeling, how to cope, and if we're expecting too much of ourselves in the process. Sacrificing your body, your relationship, or your mental health for a fairytale, for a baby, for or parenthood can be a difficult and worthwhile path just don't go too far.

CHAPTER 12:
YOU MATTER.

In life, we need to account for change. If the life you live makes you happy then, consider this a win. Stop beating yourself over the idea of a perfect existence. No one is happy all the time, my friend. Look at Jim Carey in "The Truman Show", he got so sick of perfection and repetition he tried to escape it for real emotion.

Think about how scary it must've been to go through that door? Well, he did it. I know that it's a movie, but think about all the moments in your life where you felt so bored you didn't know what to do with yourself? Or, how about those moments where you can't stand one more day of the same thing over and over? Or, what about those in which you crave attention so much that you don't care if it comes in the form of contention? He risked everything he had to have real conflict, problems, anxiety, and emotion because perfection was not satisfying. It felt wrong. It felt off. It was stifling him.

Right now, chances are you've had all the anxiety and emotion you'll need for some time. However, the magic escape door is not going to appear with a route to an alternate universe containing your Happily Ever After.

If you're holding on to that dream, please refer back to stage four. Either way, it is important that you learn life is not all sunshine and roses. Thinking that it should be is likely to wilt your dreams and leave you feeling dead. The sooner you accept life as a series of fortunate and unfortunate events, the sooner you will understand that being happy and sad are a part of the deal.

A part of this life-deal we're living is to go through it all. It requires that we make room for all of the emotions, the good *and* bad, and find a way to make it work for you. These days, people suggest self-help books to convince you a pot of happiness exists at the end of a rainbow and, to reinforce this, you must stare in a mirror and repeat something like, "I'm a Lion."

I hate to downplay your positive affirmation activities but here's a secret about that shit: it only works if you connect to it. If you don't connect to it, no amount of reading or chanting is going to make you believe it.

Happiness does not materialize by roaring in a mirror or telling yourself that you're a lion and because you're a lion everything is awesome. The fact is you will never be a lion and sometimes life sucks a giant dick! I'm sorry if you're feeling ferocious but I'm about to rain on your gleeful parade when I tell you being mad is allowed and is actually necessary to knowing when you feel happy.

When we understand the difference between feeling empowered and like you are walking around covered in poop, we understand how strong we are and how to appreciate our resilience. When we learn to appreciate our ability to live through tough shit is when we really start believing in our strength and that happiness can exist even in life's shittiest moments. Ultimately, your value is not found when things are going your way; your value lives in how you respond when the going gets tough and if you decide to keep going.

~

Tough Love: Suffering occurs when the emotions are all about you. I hate to burst your bubble but this isn't Charlie and the Chocolate Factory. It's not a good look for you to run around like Veruca Salt, screaming, "Don't care how; I want it now!"

No one is going to turn over the keys to a magic door, even if it doesn't exist, with you running around act like a little shit. Healing occurs when you learn where you can shift a pattern of obsessing over perfection to finding value and being able to give value.

You and your experiences are valid simply for no other reason than you lived them. If you don't learn from them, then you are wasting an experience. Pause for a moment with me. Think about all that you've gone through. It's some pretty heavy shit. Now, think about your niece, your sister, your best friend, or some super amazing stranger you met in the checkout line of a grocery store who happened to be really nice to you. If you discovered they were also going through this would you want them to suffer or would you want them to learn and to find their value?

In understanding your value, you examine your responsibility to your reality. When we consider how culpable we are to identifying our value, we see how to proceed. We understand what we want to be in alignment with. We decide if what we are in or out of alignment with makes us feel good and how feeling this way or not contributes to being happy.

Understanding what we want to be in energetic alignment with is not easy. It requires that you take a good long and hard look at yourself to decide if you like who you are being about your life and if you don't, deciding if you're willing to change.

It's likely you will get frustrated with your truth. It's like you will become compounded by what you uncover about yourself. Hell, it is even like that you fail getting into alignment with who you want to be before you succeed.

I cannot guarantee it will be easy to change who you are being about your life any more than it will be to face that you actually need to be different, act different, think different, and take responsibility differently for it all to change. I can, however, guarantee you there is no magic door that will take you there.

There is no magic path of how to get from point A to point Z in understanding who you are in this life, what makes you happy, and what won't make you happy. I can tell you there is one thing is for certain that will get you from where you are now to where you want to be and that is change.

No one who wanted be, think, and feel different got anywhere by standing still and doing the same thing over and over. To understand how to believe in your value, you need to come to terms with who you are now and how you feel about it. You need to decide if you like how things are going. You need to decide if in order to have your energy shift into being a happier, purposeful, driven, empowered, lovable, and loved version of you, if you can decide to allow your energy to be different? No matter what, the question you need to address is: can you allow yourself to see what it is you want to change to be happy?

CHAPTER 13:
YOU DECIDE.

Happiness is not something you purchase at the bookstore. It is not in a book. It is not in a car. It is not in a house, a job, a relationship, or a baby. It is a commitment. It is a choice. It is an embodiment. Healing is the very same thing.

No one can give you the keys to healing your hurt. You can seek help or advice, but what reinforces healing is your willingness to be it. It's not in your choice to heal that helps us do it. It is in our commitment of who we want to be about our lives, our energy, relationships, or spirits that allows us to be about it.

When you evaluate what you love about those in your life, who influences you, or why something inspires you, what do you think?
Do you think about their children?
Do you wonder if they're married?
Do you consider their favorite color?

I'm willing to bet the answers to the above are no. You think about the value they bring to your life. You wonder about challenges faced and how they survived. You consider the qualities they have that you respect and admire and how you can institute those behaviors to emulate their greatness.

We value others for the contributions they bring to our lives. Whether or not someone is married, has a child, or likes the color blue has no bearing on the value they bring to you.

For instance, my brother has 2 children. This has no bearing on my life. Gasp. Shock. Horror. Alas, it is true.

The fact that he has 2 children is lovely. I love being their Aunt. I get up every morning and tend to myself, my values, all the hard shit I have in my life so I can be a better Aunt to them and encourage them to believe in their overall badassery. However, I do not have to get up at 2 AM when my nephew has a fever because my brother does. Nope. Sorry, bro. Good luck with the thermometer, I'll be getting my sleep-on. That fever has no direct bearing on my life.

I do not have to shop for diapers because my niece is all out. Nope. I love you, but I honestly never think about whether or not she even shits. Point is you cannot diminish your relationships with others to things like marriage, child bearing or parenting, any more than they can diminish their relationships with you to those same things. Do not identify yourself as being partner-less, childless, or valueless.

Identifying your value needs to be a priority. Here's why. Your value is a key factor in being able to talk about struggling with infertility without falling into a weeping puddle on the ground. It will also prevent you from crying over baby magazines in the grocery store during check-out or saying the word *baby* without stuttering. Essentially, understanding who you are, what you're capable of, what you can and can't be with, and who you want to be in this life will keep you in check. How do you do that? Find a way to fall in love with all the things about you that bring you joy and bring you pain.

I'm not saying that loving yourself will make you impenetrable to hurt, sadness, anger, depression, or fear, but I am saying that it will give you the skills necessary to make a rebound if and when those heavy emotions arise. It will give you clarity on your self-worth. It will allow you to recognize your humanity with compassion and empathy. It will give you the strength to appreciate all the things about you that are great and not so great. It will even gift you the ability to admire the charm of you instead of leaving it as a factor determined by society.

Finding our value gives us the ability to appreciate all sides of ourselves. It gives us awareness that being human means being flawed and accepting those flaws as nothing more than a part of us. It allows us to love the beauty in them and in turn, ourselves.

~

Love is the answer to everything. I hope you agree. If not, you'll have to suffer through the next few pages in agony.

When we are in a place where we understand our value, we start to truly accept our reality. If you struggle with infertility, it doesn't make you a freak, ugly, less intelligent, or undesirable. It means you may not have a kid and in some instances, it means you just don't have one right *now*.

It also means you don't have early morning feedings, sleepless nights, unless maybe you drank too much, and days where you need to call off work for no other reason than you want to. For all those reasons that don't involve parenthood, to some capacity you can say hurray and, some days, you will relish in those things. However, pleasure over non-parenting may take some time. It could come in the next 5-minutes, 4 months, or even 10 years, but if you are committed to finding it, it will appear.

Things you can ask yourself to determine your value?
What makes me a good person? If you don't like yourself, it is unlikely anyone else will like you either. Sit and write-out 3 things about you that make you a decent human being. What qualities do you have to offer to yourself and others that you would seek in someone else? Understanding the subtle differences we bring to any given scenario is what makes you, you and, consequently, all the things that make you, you is what makes you so great! No one else is you. Share that shit!

Why would I want to be my friend? If you are a wet blanket to be around, no fun, can't enjoy anything, and find life to be more of an annoyance than occasion, you need to get out more and see the world. Sit and write-out the top 3 things you like to do and then look for those qualities in other people or where you can do these yourself and meet other people. Finding ways to get out and enjoy life is a great way to actually enjoy your life.

How can I learn to be better everyday? If you never challenge yourself, you will never grow. Sit and write-out 3 things you would like to do but intimidate you and see if you can find people to do those things with. Often times, encouragement is what we lack in execution. Finding ways to challenge yourself and surround yourself with people who force you to level-up will keep you growing and finding value in trying new things, meeting new people, and engaging in new experiences. Being a recluse will keep you closed in and restless. Get out and enjoy newness and excite yourself!

Things you can expect if you don't determine your value.

Baby showers will be a bitch! Talk about ripping the "Baby Band-Aid" off. This fucker will come off and take with it the whole scab. Ever see someone break down into an emotional wreck in the middle of a baby shower and people celebrating the 50th box of diapers, onesies, bottle cleaning contraptions, and oh no, two diaper genies, whatever will we do? Yeah. Me neither. Let's not make this you.

Christmas/holidays may give you a run for your emotional wallet. The holidays are an inevitable time of emotion overload. Relatives who you infrequently visit for a reason are overstaying their welcome. Grandparents are asking inappropriate questions at an ungodly volume. People are fucking like their heat is never coming back on and last years' "Guess who's pregnant!?" will be there with their baby in the 'baby's first Christmas' onesie. Santa Claus is coming to town and we don't need you getting kicked-out of Christmas as the Baby-Grinch Who Stole Christmas.

Keep your parenting judgment in check. There is nothing worse than someone who has no business giving advice, giving advice. Am I right? It's kinda like someone who has children telling a stressed-out couple struggling with infertility to "relax and it will happen". If you didn't catch on there, keep re-reading this until you do. Shutteth thy mouth.

Value of self is like breathing. If you don't know your worth, you are off kilter and anything that anyone says or does to you can set you off. In which case, anything you say or do can and will be held against you. Evaluate your worth and understand it, appreciate who you are, because you don't want to be the only member of the family uninvited to everything, forever, because your observations became emotional outbursts.

Infertility is a sensitive topic and your value may be impacted. Let us not become insensitive to the feelings of others simply because we have become overwhelmed by being with our own.

Infertility is infertility. You can't change it; no matter how badly I want to change it for me, I want to change it for you. I wish I could say I read somewhere that infertility was on the decline and that the Matrix is a real thing and we really can create our own reality to be what we want but we can't. If you are struggling with infertility, I can't take this away nor can I compose a sentence with enough swear words or witty puns to make the hurt die. All I can say is I hope you hear my heart when I say I wish I could.

From my entire self, I wish infertility wasn't a *thing*. I wish we didn't share in this pain. I wish there was some way to make it all go away, but I cant and you can't either. What I will say, is that I want you to know that whatever your struggle, I already love you, and all the reasons you have for being sad and all those you have for wanting to not be sad anymore.

By now, you are aware that you are the only hope you have to recover from this. There will be moments of regurgitated disappointments as well as newfound solace but your struggle is whatever you decide it to be.

You can redefine yourself anytime you want. You do not need to label yourself "barren" any more than you need to look down or feel embarrassed when you tell someone the reason you do not have children is because you can't. You didn't choose this for you. It just happened. There is nothing to be ashamed of but there is no amount of strong emotion that's going to heal this for you. You must heal this yourself. You must decide you are a valuable part of this world and you must own that your legacy is you. It is not a child. It is not a job. It is not a sports car, house, or dollar amount in your bank account. Those things can be a part of it, but that is not all there is. Your legacy is the impact you make on the lives of your family, people you meet, and the impact you make on You.

You must be impactful on your own life. You must become so completely obsessed with it that you can't imagine living any other way or as anyone else. If you want to have a baby and be a parent, I get it and there are options available, but if you feel like you've lost yourself and you don't know who you are anymore, you must become clear about who you are going to be in this struggle first.

Acceptance means giving a fuck and giving a fuck has led you here. If in a few days, months or years, you find yourself still grieving a life that was never yours to begin with, sit down with a box of Kleenex coated with aloe (or two, depends how long you've been holding this shit in) and cry a river.

There is no one in the universe with the power to tell you to just "Get Over It" because you know that is not going to get you through it. Feeling this shit, like a punch in the gut, is what will give you emotional Navy Seal survival skills for the next thing that comes your way.

Sometimes this life is a shit-show but we can show-up in our best threads looking fresh to death and choose who you are going to be about it. You still have the opportunity to decide that you can get through anything even when just the idea of it scares you. The fact is, it's more likely that there will be more things in life that will shake you to the core than don't. I do not know how many more but the point is, if this is the first time you find yourself tested and you've taken reading this book as your step to seek help or are already preparing to re-read stages 1-5, give yourself some credit. A lot of people go through very intense situations and never seek help. Congratulations, you're a human who actually gives a fuck! I'm very happy to know you.

CHAPTER 14:
TAKE CARE OF YOU.

Giving fucks is sneaky. It means being forced to ride an emotional rollercoaster each and every time it presents itself. The emotional rollercoaster to infertility does not stop after you've processed negative feelings about the situation. The emotional rollercoaster will continue on. Some days you will feel great. Others you're back to beating on yourself while wondering how you got back on this goddamn rollercoaster. Even 5-years from now when you feel like you got your emotions on lock, it's likely you will have a twinge of guilt, pain, or sadness. I've had it sneak up on me. You may too. Feelings are unpredictable and that's just how feelings go. They can be healed but they'll never truly be forgotten.

To help you through intermittent highs and lows, here's five ways I keep my mind, body, and soul sober when I am riding my emotions.

Exercise. For me, Yoga is all about calming your mind, becoming in tuned with your body, and focusing on how you feel. This physical practice is a great way to give your mental space a chance to relax from all the thinking we do. Not only is Yoga a great way to quiet your thoughts to find focus but it is also naturally healing for your body, using endorphins to decrease stress, open-up your respiratory and blood circulation, as well as releasing muscle tension.

I suggest Yoga because it is a fluid motion exercise. It is not jarring in motion like some High Intensity Interval Training or Crossfit programs and the fluidity helps to decrease tension and inflammation you may already experience depending on your infertility diagnosis. For instance, if you struggle with endometriosis, you do not need anything to contribute to inflammation. Yoga will help minimize inflammation.

How often do I do Yoga? I try to do Yoga 3-4 times per week for no more than 1 hour.
What kind of Yoga do I like? Vinyasa. It has a slow flow with steady movement.
Where do I do Yoga? In my home office, which is basically a 6ft by 6ft space or in a class.
Where can you find Yoga? Google. YouTube. If you're not comfortable going to a class, I recommend getting the Asana Rebel app on your phone and start there. If you want to jump out of your comfort zone, head to a Yoga class; the instructors will be receptive to your level of practice -even if it is, I only bend over and touch my toes to shave my ankles - they can help you with body positioning.

Eat clean, whole foods. Eating clean is almost a "negative" terminology these days because it is often incorrectly used. I am not a dietician so I won't get into the molecular and chemical advantages of not eating McDonald's everyday but, because I love you, I will tell you not to do that.

Eating clean means eating non-fertilized, natural, and organic foods from the earth as often as possible. 6 months after changing to an organic lifestyle that completely obliterated dairy, gluten, and processed foods, I discovered I was sleeping better, having prolonged energy, and my husband confirmed, I was less grumpy. Eating organic is another source for your diets' essential vitamins and minerals.

Common things I removed from my diet? Whites - sugar, bread, whole pasta, whole milk, and flour. As well as beer, the fermentation process in beer is often done with inorganic yeast and grains, which mean you're likely consuming processed things. Where I shop? Whole Foods but, in the spring and summer months, you can find me at a local food stand or farmer's market to buy all my organic veggies, fish and meats.

Common words to look for in your food? Non-GMO, Gluten Free, Organic, Grass Fed, and Cage Free. I am not a dietician but, if you see these words on the product, it's probably better for you than anything you'll ever order at a drive-thru.

Common words to avoid in your food? ANYTHING YOU CANNOT PRONOUNCE. If you find the item you're about to place in your body for digestion and absorption looks like all the consonants of the alphabet have been thrown together for shits and giggles, don't eat that shit. For instance, Butylated Hydroxyanisole. "Butylated"? This sounds like something that requires latex gloves and a downward facing dog. Personally, I don't want any of that near my mouth.

285

How do you know what you'll like? You won't. It's all trial and error. I'm not even saying you have to eat clean all the time. I am saying you need to be eating clean more than you are eating McDonalds. Just as I am not a dietician, alas, I am also not a chef. So, in the spirit of rebellion for all those nights you sat at the dinner table until you finished what was on your plate, I suggest you have fun and play with your food! If you don't like it, don't eat it! Keep trying things until you find something you do like... more often clean foods and less often from McDonald's.

Personal Development (PD). For several years, I associated Personal Development with crazy people. I thought, if you're reading a self-help book then you must have some serious shit messed-up with you. Kazah! It turns out I was right. I'm sure I'll get all kinds of shit for this one but the point is, if you feel like you need some help, motivation, or ideas on how to advance your self-perception, then reading personal development is exactly what you need.

I didn't start reading PD until I had discovered I began to feel lost and, ultimately, all kinds of fucked-up. I didn't really know what I wanted or what to read so I took suggestions from friends and from the little stars on Amazon to make uneducated guesses. Turns-out the first one was a goldie. It was, 'You Are A Badass' by Jen Sincero.

Telling you that this is a great fucking book is an understatement. She makes no excuses for herself or her past behaviors nor her present ones. It was exactly what I needed and I'm pretty sure it says fuck, shit, damn and hell almost as many times as I do here.

What are some golden PD nuggets I suggest? Well, if you like this book then you'll love the following; You Are A Badass, Do Cool Shit, The Subtle Art of Not Giving a Fuck, Get Your Shit Together, Unfuck Yourself and Happy Bitch.

Are there any I like without cuss words in the titles? Sure. I Am That Girl, Eat That Frog, Go For No, Show Your Work, How to Steal Like An Artist, Love Warrior, The Last Lecture, and The Purpose Driven Life.

How do I recommend you find what works for you? Well, you're going to need to do some internal thinking about what or where you are trying to get motivated. Is it self-confidence? Is it being more assertive? It is branching-out and achieving new dreams? Once you find what you're looking for, I recommend entering that information into Google with "self-help" or "personal development books" and scan away.

How do I find mine? As I said, I take recommendations but I find anything that talks above my head makes me fall to sleep. If you're talking about how to "lighten your load" and "live a euphoric existence", almost instantly I'm snoozed. If you're telling me to pull up my skirt and find my balls to get my shit together, then now we're talking. My Google searches look like this, "Personal Development Books with Swear Words", and so far I haven't been let down yet. I'm pretty simple when it comes to what makes me happy and it's people who are unafraid to be smart and use colorful language. That's fucking euphoria if you ask me!

~

You've taken on as much emotional turmoil as you can handle and handle it you did. Aside from getting a little emotionally drunk and belligerent, you have dealt with enough feelings of fear and grief to last you a lifetime and you have tackled it as well as anyone could expect. Essentially, you have or are battling infertility and survived. I don't know about you but that sounds pretty badass. Despite the fact that you're processing your future at this point and ingesting feelings of how to take action into a sustainable and manageable life that simultaneously gives you the ability to belly laugh and mean it, aftershocks of infertility can be anticipated for the rest of your life. It is a part of acceptance.

Acceptance is not a "Baby Band-Aid". You can't lay acceptance over deep-seated emotion and expect what's underneath to disappear. If you were expecting that, I'm sorry to disappoint you. Truth is your acceptance will need to be a continual process. It will keep you attuned to your emotions but it will also keep you honest about your feelings and receptive to processing them about infertility and other emotional things that come in the future.

Acceptance is a strong emotion. It's a beaming bright light. It allows you to acknowledge the emotions you've gone through and appreciate how you got to this place.

I realize shock, anger, depression, bargaining, and grief are not the greatest emotions. People don't line-up for rejection and despair, saying, "Please sir, may I have another?" However, the strongest and most resilient people have gone through hardships in life, accepted their presence, processed painful emotions, and come out on the other side ready to kick all the ass.

Acceptance gives you power to fearlessly acknowledge where you came from, why you needed to go through it, and, here it comes, allows you to appreciate that you did. It will not only teach you to value your struggle but also love yourself for the strength it took to endure. Once you go through something as powerful and painful as infertility, you keep what it taught you on reserve.

However you arrive at acceptance, you will notice you're not the same person anymore. Infertility will undoubtedly change you. While the journey has been difficult, it wasn't impossible and the person you were when you started is not the same. Whatever your process for healing, I hope you treat infertility like an uninvited life altering guest who's unexpectedly come to town and tells you it's going to stay a while. When this happens, hopefully, you go straight to your reserve and serve it emotional ass-kicking stages one to five, teaching it what's-up.

Through acceptance, you learn to value struggle for what it teaches you and appreciate yourself for being resilient and not giving up when it got hard. Through acceptance you find your self-worth again. Through acceptance you will be able to hear the words Baby, Baby shower, Pregnant, Expecting, Due Date, Onesie, Barren, Infertility, and not feel jilted. Through acceptance, you find peace in knowing that although you have grieved a dream life, you can still believe in the magic of having a unique fairytale all your own.

You are stronger than you think. I already love you. Do not give-up on you or your fairytale because while infertility sucks you don't!

CHAPTER 15:
THE SPRINGBOARD TO
HAPPINESS.

One of the most emotionally profound books I've read in a long time is "Love Warrior" by Glennon Doyle. The book is layered with complex emotion about the author's self-discovery and how she arrived at peace when she learned to love herself just as she is.

In the book she details how she found her voice through writing. She explains how realizing who she is in this world and as a writer contributed to her growth and personal change. I, of course, can relate to this.

Of her relationship to self and writing, she wrote, "When you write your truth, it is a love offering to the world because it helps us feel braver and less alone." When I read this sentence, I felt it reverberate like sounds of a steel drum through my soul.

The truth and value in her words struck me hard, because I realized that what she said is what I have done. I have been writing to release me from my isolation. I have been writing to find comfort and feel empowered in my mind, body and soul. I have been writing to embrace and release love, become aware of judgment, and acknowledge that vulnerabilities are what make us human, give us connection, and ultimately, is what make us, well, us.

If someone approached me today, and asked me to consider all that I've learned struggling through infertility over the past 5+ years, I'd just hand them this book and let the pages speak to them however they do. That's not to say I wouldn't talk to a person, because I have and I do and I will continue to, so if you see me don't duck and cover, and expect me to throw you a book. It's to say that nothing has been more cathartic for me than writing this to you. Nothing has changed me or given me more empathy, compassion, or self-awareness, love and connection, as putting into words the severity and complexity of this disease. Nothing has felt as honest, liberating, and revealing. It's been a humbling and transformative experience.

While this book is written from my experience and perspective, I wrote it with one intention and one only, that is to connect with anyone in the world who feels the way that I did and sometimes, often still, do; alone. It is to invite you to find release from your struggle and experience it fully, whatever that means. It is to acknowledge that what you're going through is tough, but so are you. It is to say that if you have been looking for permission to feel however you do, get messy, and acknowledge, "I don't want to do this anymore" or "I need a break" or "I need to find myself" or "Something has to change", access granted.

Today is the opportunity you have been waiting for to find yourself, forgive yourself, and learn from you. Everyday is a chance for that, but it can only be done if you are committed to it. It is attainable when we are willing to relinquish control. It is accessible when we realize there is no "owners manual" to life, so our commitment to living it as ourselves is a persistent and consistent choice that we must make everyday. It is accepting that whomever we are in the face of whatever happens is choice.

Do I still have moments where I feel challenged by infertility? Yes. You're damn right I do.
Do I still have moment where I wish I would wake-up and discover this was a dream? Absolutely.
In fact, if someone where to ask if I would prefer to change the experience and instead, have had everything go my way? I would say, yes!

I presume you were expecting me to say, No. *I would keep everything exactly the same. I've learned so much. I'm glad this happened to us.* Yadda... yadda... yadda. No. I wouldn't say that and if you find this upsetting, I am sorry to disappoint you.

I acknowledge that keeping our story exactly the same would make for some really strong storytelling. It might support my message about self-value and appreciating who you are. It would probably make for a really impactful ending too, but this isn't a fairytale. Remember? This isn't going to wrap-up neat with a bow. The fairy godmother doesn't make it all better. Sorry, guys. Maybe she lost my address, but that's just not my truth.

The truth is I *would* choose to have things be different. I would undoubtedly jump at the opportunity to see how things could have turned-out had having a baby been a joyous experience. Hell, I would still consider it a win if we were forced to endure the entire experience again, but after one of the many IUI attempts we actually got pregnant. Absolutely, I would!

Yes. I've learned so many lessons about life through infertility.
Yes. I have developed an inner strength, peace, and self-love that are stronger and more resilient than ever.
Yes. I have tapped into my heart and have discovered an ability to be vulnerable with others in a way that I have never known.
Yes. I am more connected to myself and like myself, like never before.

This is all very true. However, it would also be true that if I had the option to go back and see what life could have been like had everything gone my way, I would choose it.

Maybe it's the Life Coach in me that allows me to remain perpetually curious. Maybe it's my love for magic and a propensity to believe that anything is possible. Maybe its because I know what it's like to endure all that is this struggle. I know how it will play out. I know how proud I am of this Shannon, and in this moment, I no longer loathe myself, but I would be lying if I said I would turn down the opportunity to explore the other side. Of course I would do it. I would do it in "It's a Wonderful Life" second.

Does that mean I live longing to change things? No. No, I do not.

Everything I said and have said before is true. It's unfair that this happened to us, but I cannot make it different. I cannot continue to be at war with my body and lose myself at the same time. I cannot and I will not. I choose to believe that it does not serve me to rest in those feelings. Instead, I believe in fate and destiny.

I believe that this was my journey to take. I believe that I was meant to travel this road with none other than Scott and that there is a force bigger than me that knew he and I, together, could take it. I'm not saying that I like it, but I am saying I accept it and I am grateful that we were able to get to where we are now. I accept it but I don't have to disengage what's in my heart and that is, I will never be grateful this happened, just as I will never abandon the feelings of love I already have for our child.

A part of that acceptance means that this experience, and the pain it brought me, will never leave. It's mine. I own it, but I will not let it make me miss the life I have to live today. I will not let it make me believe that I am unworthy of a child, that I would be a terrible Mother or that I am atoning for something, which I may never be fully aware. I cannot and will not continue to engage those thoughts. It doesn't mean they won't pop-in to say "Hi" from time to time, but my awareness to them now is different. I am aware that they exist and I love on them when they do. Whereas before, when they showed-up, I judged myself for having them and used them to amplify my guilt and confine me to sadness.

I know there will always be a part of me that hopes *this is the month* we get our miracle. That believes my 'fairytale' life involves having our child. I also know that while the hope exists in my mind and heart, I can visit those feelings without guilt or resentment and love them for what they are, because that is what I choose.

I know that I love my husband. I loved him before the idea of a child and I will love him with or without one.

I know that I love myself. I loved myself enough to give my body over to the unknowns of creating a life, and I will love who I am whether I do or do not have a child.

I love who we both have been individually in this struggle, and together. I am proud of us for all the ways in which we have endured and survived this burden and I am grateful that we made it to the other side. In all of that knowing, I don't feel the need to push myself any further right now. I do not feel that my husband and I are any less of a family because we do not have a child. I choose to create the joyous, fulfilled, and purpose driven life I seek, and right now, I don't feel the need to have a child to do it.

A lot has changed since our initial diagnosis. Who Scott and I are as people, but also our marriage, our friendship, the way we communicate, the risks we're willing to take and the things we want or declare we do not. I feel stronger than ever in our relationship and that is because I feel stronger within myself.

Infertility changed me. I have changed me. Through the experience in total, I have transformed. I struggled, learned, and survived, in the face of wanting a child, and knowing that I still want one, but will not allow it to define me, is growth. It allows me to know that the yearning may never go away and that doesn't have to be bad. It can be beautiful, because while I still want it, it's not because I can't have it, and while I don't have it, the value I find in loving me no longer exists within the confines of infertility.

To date, I am the strongest, most loving, and beautiful, grateful, and badass version of myself I have ever been. I can't take all the credit for this. I have to applaud and send sincere gratitude to all the friends, family, and loved ones who were unwavering and generous with their unending love and support. As much as I would like for things to be different, to have had the path been easier, to not have faced the deepest and darkest parts of myself, I believe it has all been for a reason; so that I would have the opportunity to meet this version of me and dammit if I don't just love her so much!

Yes. The path to where I am now has been filled with anger, depression, and grief. Yes. It has tested the strength of my relationships, including the one I have with myself. Yes. I have gained new connections and lost old ones along the way. Yes. It has been very enlightening and uplifting, but it has also been lonely and dark, but not to the point where I feel bitter about it. In fact, infertility taught me how much I love the dark and maybe I always have.

I believe that without the dark moments in our life we would have far less appreciation for the light. That in the moments where nothing makes sense we have an opportunity to see how beautifully complex and intrinsically messy life can be.

When the moments where nothing seems to be going right persist, and life feels ominous, there is also a bit of mystery, mystique, and electric energy. It can be scary and unpredictable, but it can also be liberating and free. For all these reasons, I can't help but wonder if the darkness led me to my pain and through it I have been able to find love and light. If perhaps, it is why I am able to see my hurt as something to hide and instead use it to learn from, grow with, and love.

Maybe I needed to learn that there is no such thing as control.
Maybe I needed to learn that all we can do is trust that whatever happens we can handle it.
Maybe I needed to discover that happiness is not our purpose; that connecting to the real, true, and uninhibited value within us is.
Maybe I love Tinkerbell, magic, and believed in fairytales, with such liberty, because I know that my attachment to light and happiness, is equal to my connection with sadness and the dark.
Maybe I welcome the dark, because I've always been curious about the depths of my own, but never found reason to explore it.
Maybe I needed to go through all of this to finally understand who I want to be in this world.
Maybe I needed to accept my courage.
Maybe I needed to see the depths of my strength.
Maybe all of it is the same for me as it is for you.
Or, perhaps the truth is we will never know.

We will never truly understand why we are on this journey or any journey for that matter. The best we can do is try. Try to find the value and meaning within all of life's circumstance. Try to trust our choices and give space to our feelings. Try to believe that we are capable of overcoming anything and consistently, commit to all of that with integrity.

~

I see now that I withheld love from myself on our journey. I look back on everything that has happened over the past few years and what I conclude is that there was no space for love in a place where I blamed, hated, and judged myself. I wanted to be mad, but I didn't know who to be mad at, so I became mad at me. I decided that if I couldn't fix infertility and find joy, love, and release within it, then I would hold onto what was right there in front of me; pain.

Looking back, I realize there is no such thing as feeling only pain or only love. They are a package deal. They are both things that we have the capacity to feel and to put them in opposition of each other is to pretend that we must choose to have one without the other. It doesn't have to be that way and in my opinion, it actually isn't.

Pain and love are like the light and the dark. When it comes to being present to either one, our awareness is there because we have been exposed to both. We know what pain feels like because we have experienced love. Conversely, we know what love feels like because we have withstood pain. One can make us feel happy while the other can make us feel sad and somewhere along the way we decide that one is better.

When faced with the option to be *happy* or *sad* I think that most of us would undeniably choose happy. We look at attaining happiness as a victory; something we fought for and won, and so we surrender to it with ease. We welcome it and everything associated, to wash over us with belonging and purpose. We nestle into its warmth like a clean, blanket, which is fresh out of the dryer. We love happy and let it love us right back! However, when it comes to sadness, pain, or regret, well... that's a-whole-nother story.

We run from pain. We hide from it and in most cases, I would dare to say we do everything in our power to reject and avoid it. It's not wrong. It's just something we do because we decide that it doesn't feel the same as happiness, joy, and love. We decide it is not something we want to be with.

It doesn't make us feel like we've accomplished anything. It doesn't feel fresh, warm, and new. It feels like we've failed or lost, and so we fight it. We deny it. We reject surrendering to it. We do everything in our power to refuse its presence; all the while knowing it is still there. It is just as strong and present as all those "good" feelings too.

We refuse pain because we're afraid of what it *means* if it is given space, time, and recognition. We're afraid of what it will do to us if we surrender to it with ease, welcoming it to have belonging and purpose. We don't allow it to be cozy and comforting, because we decide that it is scary and lonely. We decide that we won't like what it has to say, do, or how it will feel.

Instead of giving pain the opportunity to be a thing that loves and teaches, it becomes the hairy, scary, monster that lives under your bed. It becomes the thing that if it gets a hold of you, will sink its tentacles into you, and suck you dry from the inside out like a raisin. Long story short, somewhere along the way we decide, happy = good, while pain = bad, ingesting a feelings based problem and deconstructing it to find a solution with algebra. Also known as using your head to solve a heart based problem.

We welcome love and fear pain based on how we define it. We decide that we know and like what brings us happy feelings, so we create space to be with them and label them as *good*. We decide that we don't care to neither know nor like what make us feel sad, so we avoid it, pretend it's not there, and label it as *bad*.

We take the good with the bad and put them at odds with each other. When we do this, we also put feeling, and how we choose to manage it or not, at odds within us too. We create an internal war that begins with "I only want to strive for good because I like it" and "I refuse the bad because I don't". It's a lose-lose scenario that keeps us disconnected from fully being who we are and pretending that life will only be worth living when things are going *good*, and leaves us living a life that is only 1/2 as good, 1/2 the time.

Accepting who, where, and what we are in our lives can be intimidating. Accepting that we're messy can be daunting. Accepting that we're complicated and that sometimes being complicated is what gives living that electric feel can be confusing as hell! So what?

Can you be with feeling intimidated for the sake of clarity?
Can you be messy in exchange for finding your purpose?
Can you be complicated if it means you finally find the value in yourself?

Love and pain are not in opposition. One is not the winner, while the other is the loser. We decide that. It's not written in a rulebook somewhere. It is you who chooses what you will and will not allow yourself to be present to about you. It is you who decides who you are or not, and what you can or cannot be with about yourself.

Love is not an ooey-gooey, good, warm, and welcoming feeling. It does show-up as 12 long stem roses, an engagement ring, or having a child in a rulebook somewhere. We give it that meaning. Just as pain is not a scary, or bad and cold, failure, it isn't defined by quitting a job, divorce or infertility. Those are things that we apply to love and pain. It is all us and it is what we decide.

While it sucks to admit that we basically determine what makes us feel bad and good, it's also great because it gives us the opportunity to turn that choosing into a choice. Meaning, just as quickly as we can decide that something is painfully shitty, we can un-decide it.

It was Alfred Lord Tennyson who said, "Tis better to have loved and lost, then never to have loved at all." It's very easy to see the love in all of what he mentions in that one sentence, but I tend to think that's because he directly states the word twice.

In this quote, what I see is him pointing to the two very things we put at odds within ourselves and others, love and pain. Becoming intimate with both *good* and *bad* feelings and knowing the sacrifice that each place on us as humans does not determine that love is better. No. I see that pain and love, happiness and sadness, good and bad, are equals and we are no better off when we have one or the other, but that we are stronger, learned, and more in alignment within ourselves for having the awareness to appreciate and experience the value of both love and loss together.

It is not predetermined that you will *like, value, or need* love more than you will pain. No. You decided that long ago. You made it mean something good when you got an A+ on that test, went on your 1st date with your crush, bought the new car, won employee of the month, paid off your student loans, got married, had a kid and successfully, installed that garage opener without any help. It was also you who made it bad when you lied, got dumped, lost your Grandmother's broach, made a poor investment, got fired, got divorced, couldn't have kids, and accidentally, backed into the garage door.

It was you who decided that feeling *happy* is infinitely better than feeling sad. It is you who labeled the good's, *good* and the bad, *bad.* It's you who labels the wins *better, ideal, or admirable* and doesn't allow pain to be a *love-learned* lesson. It is you who defines the worth, or significance of each. The power of one or the other doesn't have to be good versus evil. Who you are in the face of each doesn't have to be a leader or a loser. What you are in either scenario doesn't have to be a winner or a failure. All of it, ALL OF IT, is up to you.

~

Choice is a beautiful thing. It's not up for debate or criticism from others. It's unequivocally up to you. Infertility wasn't up to me any more than it is up to you, but how we deal with, respond to it, and label it, is.

When it comes to being with strong feelings, we don't always know how to respond and in an effort to deconstruct the emotions that we can't be with, sometimes we try to rationalize it. Sometimes we take it in as something that is happening with the heart and we try to resolve it with the head. When it becomes too complex we apply algebraic thinking of what is the quickest route through it, taking you straight from A to Z. I wish it were that simple.

I wish it were as easy as saying, simply, turn your feelings knob off and don't feel pain. However, pain is unavoidable. In my case, I determined it was justice for not producing a baby. The more I didn't get what I wanted, the more I became committed to that emotion and so it became retribution. It was what I considered a well-deserved punishment. When I accepted it as one, I held on to it. I became it. I shut off my ability to find joy, because at every turn in our journey I failed. I couldn't take us from A to Z on the baby-train and no matter how hard I was trying or how much I was investing in this process, I couldn't see it.

I couldn't see how supported I was by my friends and family, or how much they wanted to remind me, that I was worthy of love. I couldn't see that the very act of me trying endlessly to create and produce life was an act of love. I couldn't see that while the pain of the struggle was undeniable, love was there, just not for me.

I wanted to contribute the most deep and personal parts of me to the universe and in doing all of it, I was willing to become more connected to myself than ever before. I was so blinded by pain and anger that I couldn't see that everything I was doing, no matter how goal, task, or time oriented, was because I wanted to be, give, and create love. Wanting a child is an act of love. Intentionally deciding to make a baby is an act of love. Fighting infertility is an act of love. It was all an act of love for my family, my husband, the world but also myself.

~

It all makes sense – NOW. At least, it does in my head.

Falling into an abyss of sadness, isolation, self-loathing and regret, it's interesting that I didn't respond with compassion or empathy. I responded to it like it was a math problem. A + B = C. Scott's sperm + Shannon's Uterus = Baby. Also known as, the love from my husband + the love from me = the love we have for a family. Except, our equation was Scott's Sperm + Shannon's Uterus = Nothing.

How I responded was very enlightening. It isn't what I would have hypothesized when faced with a life altering experience; one that challenged my beliefs, dreams, and desires, as well my sense of self. It's enlightening to know that I didn't respond with kindness. Instead, I used rage, anger, and resentment to drive me.

I used feelings that were the exact opposite of love in order to keep going. I was using an abundance of negative energy to propel me forward. I couldn't see that I didn't need more determination, commitment, and perseverance with my fear goggles on. I could see that all of that was already there. The feelings of respect, adoration, and nurturing myself through the consistent disappointment were what was missing, and because the idea of quitting was unacceptable, compassion remained far away.

The pain didn't make the situation any more or less difficult. In fact, the pain actually made sense because it was always there. I could be smiling and pretending that everything was "fine" or clapping at a baby shower, but rage and heartbreak were there, lingering, under the surface.

I wouldn't say that the pain didn't make all that we were doing to conceive any less a valiant effort. It was all very consuming and so feeling tortured made sense. What didn't make sense, was trying to convince myself that I shouldn't or didn't need to be agonizing over this process. I was furious and enraged. Pretending like I wasn't, after everything we had done, wouldn't have changed the fact that I want a child in spite of it not working-out. I needed to feel it - all of it. I know that now.

I don't lament over feeling the pain, but I do recognize how harmful holding onto those feelings was and is. I recognize the need to go through grief and feel sorrow, but I also see that I didn't love myself through it and that's because I didn't love myself.

It probably would have helped me to see how damaging I was being to myself as it was happening. It might have even given me the opportunity to ask myself, if I wanted to have a baby at the cost of losing myself for 5 years? Yet, I couldn't see it. I didn't see it. None of that happened.

All of this considered, and given the awareness I now have about needing to be with and create space for my pain, I see love within that. I see that while it felt like I was falling down a rabbit hole and torturing myself, while also isolating myself from other people, I can also see that I needed to go through it. I needed to feel the pain, because it was true.

I was in a great deal of turmoil in my life and in my relationships, with all that I thought was unavailable to me. There was no amount of telling myself to "snap out of it" that was going to make that happen. Even though I tried that. It didn't and would never have worked. I needed to be in pain to learn how to value Shannon, to love Shannon, and how I wanted that awareness to translate in my life, relationships, and what I will or won't accept from myself and other people.

I don't know what life would be like if I had gone through this experience and chose to stay in my grief. I don't know because that is not what happened and quite honestly, I'm glad it didn't.

Looking back now, I see that while our decision to have a baby was born from love, my choice to keep going and sacrificing my well-being for as long as I did was a product of pain. It was because I chose to see them as mutually exclusive.

I had to explore my pain to understand what I was going through and love what I couldn't be with about it. What I discovered is that I was in pain and a tremendous amount of it, but I didn't know how to love myself through it. I knew what I wanted and that was to stop this pattern, I just didn't know how to forgive myself for it. I wanted to find a way to be me without all the damaging thoughts, feelings, and patterns of isolating behaviors. I was stuck in a place where I knew the *what* that I wanted, I just didn't know the *how* to go about and get it.

I didn't know *how* to break my cycle. I didn't know *how* to find the love for myself within all the pain. I didn't know *how* to crawl out of the hole I was in without carrying all of the things that made me feel *bad* with me and burying myself under it all over again.

When I realized that I didn't know the *how* but I knew the *what*, I guess you could say I made a decision that maybe it didn't have to matter. Perhaps, it didn't have to be the worst thing if I didn't know *how* I was going to get my happy back, but notice it was good that I wanted it. This desire for happiness was a foreign thought, but when I recognized it, I knew it meant that it was there. I just didn't know who I was if I wasn't struggling with infertility. I didn't know how I could make it possible for me to ever heal from something that felt so detrimental. I didn't know, again, because I didn't know *how* it would be possible to ever find out.

There was a lot I didn't know and many questions I had about who I was after infertility struck.
Who I am if I'm not struggling with infertility?
What happiness can I find without a child?
Where does that leave Scott and me?

Am I growing outside of our relationship?
How do I get any of the things that I want?

I didn't know *who* I wanted to be, but I knew that I no longer wanted to be in a constant struggle. I didn't know *how* I was going to stop this pattern, but somehow, the not knowing was OK. I didn't know *where* that left my relationships with other people, but suddenly, I mattered more.

I didn't know the *how* but I knew the *what*. I was the *what*. I wanted to find myself, who I am now after infertility. I wanted to like myself, feel sexy, smart, worthy and empowered. I wanted to stop associating to myself as this disease and look at it as something that happened to me, versus something that is me.

I decided that this thinking would be what I held onto. This would be what was going to help me take my 1st step in breaking a pattern. This is what would push me to stop living in isolation, self-hatred, & fear. This *what* would force me to stop feeling like there was no hope for the life I wanted and would allow me to make a long-lasting and sustainable change to love myself.

In life, we often feel those nudges to move, take action, transform, or to disrupt our patterns, but because we don't know how to do it, we stop, get stuck, and nothing changes. This doesn't have to be the case. This doesn't have to be the way it is. You can choose something different.

You can choose to have more faith in you than in your fear. You can choose to believe you are worthy of realizing all your happiness. You can decide that it is time to listen to that voice inside of you that is saying, "You are d*one* with doing "fine". You are ready to experience *awesome.* You are worthy of *love.* It makes sense that you would *love you.*

It's ok if you don't know the *how.* The *what* will teach you about yourself. The *what* will give you the courage, love, and will to get going and keep going. The *what* guides you to the life you love versus the life you accept. The *what* will lead you to the *how.* So, don't worry so much about the *how* now, brown cow. Sorry. I couldn't help myself. Focus on your *what.* Ask yourself what is it that you want? Once you have your answer, then ask yourself if you have the love, power, and desire in you to go out, break your pattern, and take it?

I thought I knew who I was before infertility, but infertility taught me that I was in a period of transformation in my life and come hell or high-water, I was going to go through it. It was a mess. I was a mess. The entire experience was raw. It was real. It demanded a lot of me and I fought it the whole way, but I came out on the other side a powerful woman.

I didn't enjoy the rollercoaster ride of infertility. Not one bit. But in the journey, I did find value. I found the value of self, love, and appreciating that sometimes the pain may be difficult to face, but in facing it we can allow it to teach us. We allow it to show us who we are when things are hard and life isn't rosy. We see that there is a mountain to climb and we can choose to sit down and stay down, or we can stand up and climb, but either way we will find out who we are and what we're made of.

I found everything I never knew I needed and yet, no answers to the thing I was trying to overcome, but I am still standing. I guess you could say I found no answers, but I did find myself.

I found that I could be with suffocating levels of pain, anger and resentment. I found that when faced with them I withheld kindness, compassion, and empathy from myself. I found that I'm not a very good friend to me, and doing better at that is and will continue to be my number one priority. No one will love me like I love me and I don't and won't feel bad about that. I will be fierce in my commitment to it and vulnerable in my pursuit to protect it.

Infertility is not me. It is not you. It isn't even close to being ½ of you. It is not the sum of your experience or how you respond to it. It is not a shut door or a branding. It doesn't make the rules. It doesn't call the shots and it does not define you.

This is your story. You get to decide how it goes. You get to define your acceptance. Acceptance is not where happiness lives. Acceptance is a springboard to happiness. This is not the end for me and it doesn't have to be for you. Acceptance is only the beginning.

56443223R00188

Made in the USA
Columbia, SC
25 April 2019